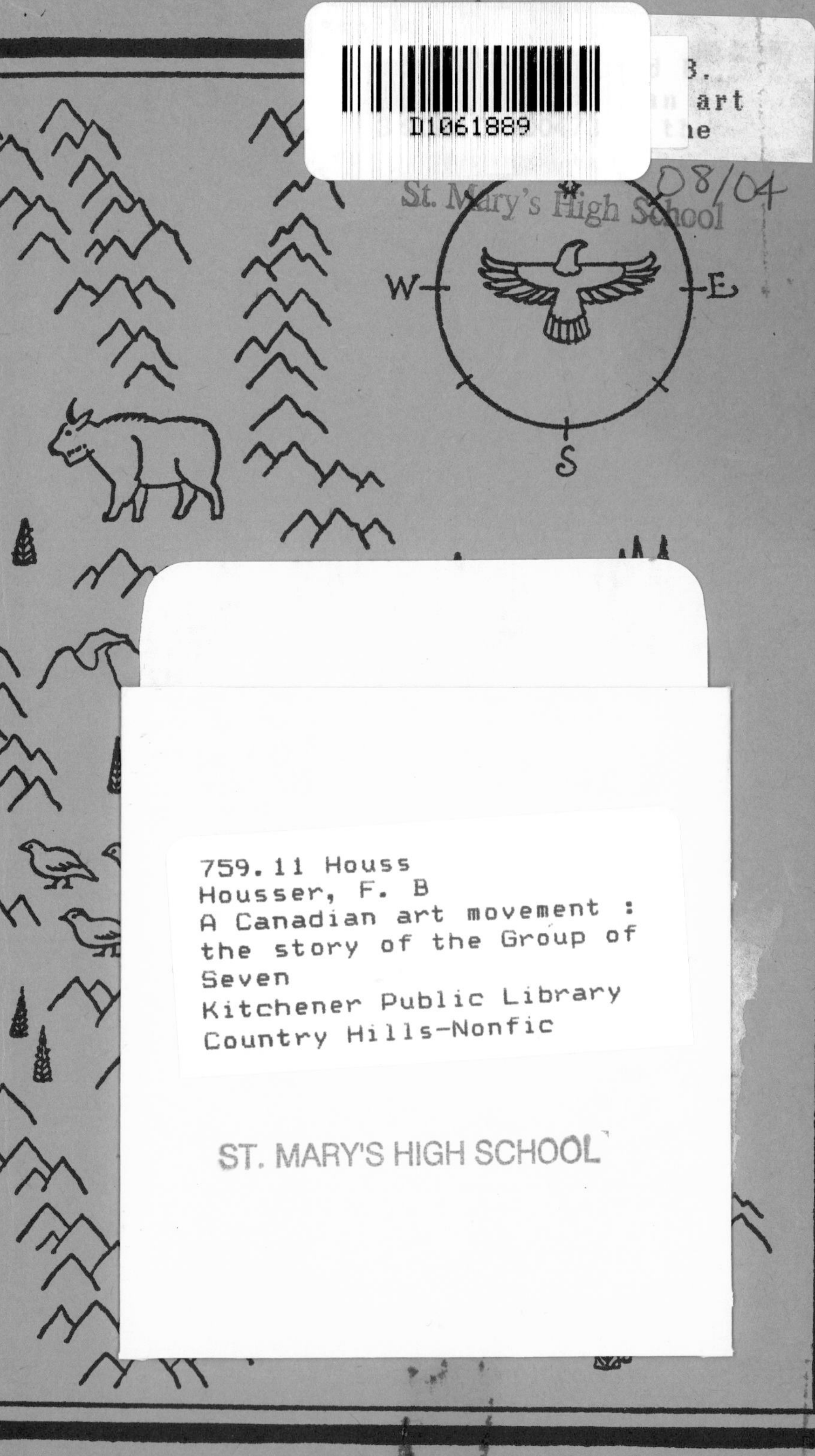
D1061889
08/04
St. Mary's High School
W
E
S
759.11 Houss
Housser, F. B
A Canadian art movement :
the story of the Group of
Seven
Kitchener Public Library
Country Hills-Nonfic
ST. MARY'S HIGH SCHOOL

A CANADIAN ART MOVEMENT

ST. MARY'S SENIOR GIRLS' SCHOOL
35 WEBER STREET WEST
KITCHENER

A CANADIAN ART MOVEMENT

The Story of the Group of Seven

BY F · B · HOUSSER

Toronto : The Macmillan Company of Canada Limited, at St. Martin's House - MCMXXVI

Copyright, Canada 1926
by F. B. Housser

This edition published 1974 by arrangement with the Estate of
F. B. Housser

ISBN 0-7705-1205-4

The jacket, title page, and endpapers
are by Thoreau MacDonald and are reproduced
exactly from the original edition.

Printed in Canada
for
The Macmillan Company of Canada Limited
70 Bond Street Toronto M5B 1X3

11892

The American bards shall be marked for generosity and affection and the encouragement of competitors. They shall be cosmos without monopoly or secrecy, glad to pass anything to anyone,—hungry for equals night and day.

WALT WHITMAN.

Contents

CHAPTER		PAGE
	Introduction	11
I.—	The Beginning	25
II.—	Lawren Harris	34
III.—	Signs of Revolt	44
IV.—	A. Y. Jackson	50
V.—	Nineteen Hundred and Thirteen	57
VI.—	In Montreal	68
VII.—	Jackson and Harris	76
VIII.—	Thomson Starts to Paint	89
IX.—	Entrenched	98
X.—	MacDonald's "Tangled Garden"	106
XI.—	Death of Thomson	115
XII.—	Mentioned in Despatches	126
XIII.—	New Materials	136
XIV.—	The Group of Seven	143
XV.—	Early Group Shows	157
XVI.—	Jackson Paints Again	163
XVII.—	Lismer	172
XVIII.—	Harris's "Above Lake Superior"	182
XIX.—	Covering Ground	193
XX.—	Spread of the Movement	204
	Some Works of the Group of Seven in Public Collections	217

A CANADIAN ART MOVEMENT

Introduction

IN the year 1910 the Royal Canadian Academy sent an exhibition of pictures to England, and a discerning critic of the *Morning Post* wrote the truth about them.

"There is," he said, "distinct evidence of two qualities which have created the masterpieces of the past, namely, feeling and observation. At present these qualities are to a great extent prevented from assuming any original form of expression because of the necessity of seeking the means of expression in the ateliers of a foreign land far from the inspiration of native history, types, and environment. At present the observation of the physical fact is strong, but the more immutable essences of each scene is crushed out by a foreign-begotten technique."

Before 1910, a Canadian art movement, inspired by Canadian environment, was not thought possible. Canadian art authorities did not believe that our rough landscape was art material. For years it had been said that pine trees were unpaintable. Our hinterlands were supposed to be too ugly as a medium of expression for a painter unless disguised to look like Europe or England. Canadian artists and the Canadian public preferred the softer, mistier, and tamer landscape of the old world. Our Canadian scenery was painted after the manner of Corot, Constable, or the Barbizon School. The view held in artistic circles in the Dominion previous to 1910, and indeed a view still widely accepted, was that Canada was a colony of Great Britain and that the colonial must needs express himself through methods approved by time and the intelligencia. To reflect our day and environment would be a vulgar adventure. "We are told we are a young country," a naughty anonymous writer once wrote to *The Canadian Bookman,* "but in art we must shun all signs of youthfulness."*

This emphasis on our youthfulness caused another misconception, still popular, that art is a sort of frill of income, age and idleness. One of our older painters, writing on Canadian art in 1913, begins his article with the observation that as yet the country had not produced a large enough wealthy class of citizens and that therefore we possessed few idle rich men's sons who might naturally drift into "dabbling" with the arts.† One could quote expres-

*This was written in 1923, showing that the ideas of Canadian art here expressed were live issues thirteen years after the period to which this chapter refers.

†*Year Book of Canadian Art.*

sions of a sentiment indicative of an attitude that is rapidly changing; a point of view which is an inheritance of colonial worship for the mother country. Our British and European connection in fact, so far as creative expression in Canada is concerned, has been a millstone about our neck. "It is necessary that as Canadians we should believe that we are as capable of producing great art as we believe we are capable of doing great deeds," says Arthur Lismer, vice-principal of the Ontario College of Art. "The imminent generation of the youth of Canada will come to produce fine art and fine craftsmanship because gradually they will become esthetically aware of their environment."‡

Science recognizes that environment affects individuals and contributes toward the creation of racial characteristics. The North American Indian, sensing presences in the mountains, trees, rocks, lakes, and rivers, worshipped them, perhaps worshipping at the same time something in himself. We do not worship Nature, but we acknowledge her influence upon us. Nature and the universe are a mystery which Science seeks to understand. Art is on the same adventure as Science, with this difference, that Science tries to comprehend Nature's body while Art tries to apprehend her spirit.

‡*Canadian Theosophist,* Feb. 15th, 1925.

ST. MARY'S SENIOR GIRLS' SCHOOL
35 WEBER STREET WEST
KITCHENER

The so-called northern wilderness of Canada has made a fringe of civilization across a continent. The wilderness has influenced our trade routes and has already undoubtedly had an effect in the formation of our racial character. This North is a magnetic land, able to get hold of men and draw them as it draws the steel of the compass. When a group of Canadian painters came, enthusiastic over the wonders and beauty of the Ontario northland, it was derogatively said by a Toronto critic, "This school of painting is not of the soil but of the rocks." But this land of rocks constitutes by far the greater portion of the total area of Canada. It is the race's inescapable environment. It is the playground of hundreds of thousands of Canadian people. The love of it is deep in our souls. To any one who has ever really been bitten by the North, the call to go back never leaves him and it is inevitable that its overpowering mood will find expression in the nation's art.

The North, like the West, creates types. It is "an indication of ourselves." The North, like the West, to be expressed in paint, demands the adapting of new materials to new methods. Brush skill and draftsmanship are not enough. A suitable soul-equipment and great powers of creative expression are essential. If you would appreciate the problem of the painter of Canadian landscape, think of the spirit of the West and of the North, then think of the task of expressing that spirit in paint on a few square yards of canvas.

This task demands a new type of artist; one who divests himself of the velvet coat and flowing tie of his caste, puts on the outfit of the bushwhacker and prospector; closes with his environment; paddles, portages and makes camp; sleeps in the out-of-doors under the stars; climbs mountains with his sketch box on his back. Possibly never before have such physical demands been made upon the artist, nor have painters been faced with so quantitudinous a mass of new material; such complexity of rhythm and design; such elemental entities in forms, the virgin mood unchastened by contact with man. In Europe, the racial spirit clings like pollen to rural and peasant pasture lands and ancient cities. In Canada the race's mood still hovers in space over the natural forms of the wilderness, and is "a thing in itself."

Painting in Europe, since Cezanne, has become a business of research and experiment, differing in these respects very little from the laboratory methods of science. As always, the mediocre painter yields willingly to the seductive influence of so-called old masters and old schools, and modern European artists who are far from mediocre, have been allured by Cezanne, whose despotism also shackles contemporary painting in the United States. Cezanne in turn, Faure tells us, was for fifteen years tyrannized over by the works of Courbet, Daumier and Delacroix. Always in Europe, "tradition," that beautifully powerful despot, gets into the saddle of the soul and curbs for at least a time the freest spirits. As long as Canada regarded herself artistically as a mere outpost of Europe; as long as her painters elected for voluntary mediocrity by the mental admission that Canadians possess no potentialities with which to create a culture as good or better than Europe's; so long was our modern twentieth-century-born spirit of independence voiceless. There is an inexorable law which says "Create or be a slave."

We need to redefine the terms "tradition" and "modern." Tradition means "to hand on," an act involving giving as much as receiving. Creation includes both. Canada is a modern by birth and her traditions are modern. It is therefore inevitable that our ultimate art expression should be modern. "Modernism" is a movement of life and is not restricted to schools of art nor methods of painting. Since Canadian confederation in 1867, an era of revaluation in art, science, religion, and life itself has taken place in the western world. This grand adventure into the unknown is sometimes said to have undermined faith. As a matter of fact, it *is* faith. The faithless are those who will not adventure from fear of losing the illusions they possess.

The critic of the *Morning Post* spoke well and truly. For Canada to find a true racial expression of herself through art, a complete break with European traditions was necessary; a new type of artist was required; a type with sufficient creative equipment to initiate a technique of its own through handling new materials by new methods; and what was required more than technique was a deep-rooted love of the country's natural environment. We do not know what mood we shall create which will be called "Canadian," but it can come only through a love of our own landscape, soil and air. We needed men devout toward their own things,—"pausers, and contemplators of tufts of blossoms"; men who at heart could concur with Whitman when he says, "Dead poets, philosophers, priests; martyrs, artists, inventors, governments long since; language-shapers on other shores,— I dare not proceed till I respectfully credit what you have wafted hither. I have perused it; own it is admirable, moving a while among it; think nothing can ever be greater, nothing can ever deserve more than it deserves. Regarding it all intently and a long while, then dismissing it, *I stand in my own place with my own day here.*"

These conditions we find rarely fulfilled in the artist personel of Canada previous to the year 1910, perhaps, as the English critic said, "because of the necessity of seeking the means of expression in the ateliers of a foreign land far from the inspiration of native history, types and environment." True, we find one or two painters in the country whose work was a gesture in a new direction, but most of them preferred to migrate to other lands and sever themselves from their native soil. If we dig back into the dim past there are traditions in Quebec of one, Frere Luc, and a succession of painters whose efforts were mostly in the way of religious pictures, some of them very accomplished. But most of them had studied abroad and they continued their work here after the manner of foreign schools. It is said that as early as 1668 Monseigneur de Laval established a school of arts and crafts at St. Joachim which produced the sculptors and architects who created many of the fine old churches along the St. Lawrence and who developed a distinctive type of architecture which belongs to the country as no later architecture does. Another art school was established at St. Vincent de Paul, near Montreal, about the year 1800, by Louis Quevillon, which was responsible for the school of woodcarvers whose spirited works are still seen in churches all over the province of Quebec, work which is scarcely appreciated to-day and which is being replaced by garish plaster casts.

About the middle of the last century Paul Kane wandered westward painting Indians and wild landscape. Kane had the necessary physical requirements of the new type of artist demanded by the country, but his pictures, a number of which are now in the Royal Ontario Museum, can scarcely be classed as works of art, their interest being archæological and historical.

Not until Kreighoff do we find a new gesture in Canadian painting and an approach to what we are in search of. Cornelius Kreighoff was born in Germany but migrated to America, married a French-Canadian and made his home in Quebec for many years. Here was a solitary early robin about whom hardly anything is known. His paintings of the Quebec habitant, the Indians and the St. Lawrence in winter are rather illustrative and pictorial, but that he could be thrilled by his adopted environment is evident in one or two of his canvases which hang to-day in the Canadian National Gallery at Ottawa and from odd sketches scattered about the country in private collections. One can become excited over some of Kreighoff's winter scenes of the early days, so painstaking and sincere. "They are Canadian classics" writes Lawren Harris, "one can wander anywhere in them and it becomes an emotionally informing experience."* Perhaps, as has been said, they are in the main literature, but there is little in Canadian writing to compare with them. Here, unquestionably, we see a direct emotional response to Canadian environment, the first to be recorded on canvas. He seems to have been interested chiefly in people. In his quaint "browny-like" peasant groups the landscape is merely a setting like the background on a stage, but there is a bleak, growling, wintry mood in some of them which does not appear in Canadian art again until Cullen began to exhibit his early out-of-door canvases about 1900. Kreighoff is a mythical figure. He must have received a certain amount of appreciation in his day for "spurious" Kreighoffs are very common, showing that his style and subjects were copied by less creative painters. His work has been pretty thoroughly ignored, but there are signs abroad to-day which make one believe that he may still come into his own. He died in Denver, Colorado, in 1880.

Our most eminent Canadian artist to date, the late J. W. Morrice, whose works hang in some of the

**The Canadian Bookman,* Feb. 1926.

most important art galleries of Europe, is better known in foreign lands than at home. He is one of those just referred to, who left the country of his birth and settled abroad where he resided for so many years that he has come to be regarded as a Frenchman. "The Irish painter, O'Connor, and the Canadian Morrice," writes Clive Bell, the English art critic, "are both known and respected in Paris, because they have lived their lives there and know none but French influences. They are rarely thought of as British."† Had he found encouragement to remain in Canada, it is difficult to speculate what final direction his work might have shown. As we shall see, he was beginning to have an influence in Montreal before he permitted Europe to absorb him. There is no doubt that he had a feeling for the landscape of his native land. A. Y. Jackson, of whom we shall hear presently, tells of visiting an exhibition in Paris in his student days. On the walls were art works of several countries. "But as I entered the gallery," says Jackson, "a small canvas in one corner of the exhibition attracted me at once. A thrill went through me. Before I knew the name of the painter or the title of the picture, I knew it was the

†Clive Bell's book *Since Cezanne*—Another writer says: "His French Colleagues paid him the highest compliment they knew, namely, of forgetting that Morrice was not a French painter."

St. Lawrence River. The painter of it was J. W. Morrice."

Morrice in exile felt and retained a fondness for his native land till he died. It is said of him that he was always particular to proclaim his nationality when occasion demanded. A writer who remembers him in Paris says, "When I first knew Morrice he occupied an apartment in an old tumble-down house, once a mansion on the Quai Les Grands Augustins and which looked out upon a scene for which he had a great love and often painted. I have an idea that when snow fell, the view reminded him of Quebec."‡

These sidelights on Morrice's character indicate real feeling for his old environment. Had he appeared as a figure in Canadian art twenty-five years later than he did, his sympathy with the modern movement in painting might have swung him into association with the group of which this book is an appreciation. As it was, his painting was inspired by quite another environment. It is rich in colour, rather sad, moody and poetic; the expression of a man buried in a world of "art for art's sake." His development passed through many stages of experimentation, his later pictures being more advanced than those of his youth. He was one of the early

‡Muriel Colkowsky in the *Canadian Forum.*

robins who came and remained for a time with us unnoticed, a harbinger of the oncoming spring.

Morrice's contemporary, Maurice Cullen, who is still painting, is another one of these early robins. His first pictures showed a break from the European tradition, especially as to subject. They had the stern vigour of the open air and along with Morrice, Cullen was one of the influences in Montreal which helped to end the domination of the omnipresent Barbizon and Dutch schools popularized by the purses of connoisseurs.

Cullen loved the country and its environment too much to run away, but although he had no end of courage, the struggle for existence seems at last to have made him compromise with his creative soul so that his work has not become the influence which it promised.

Kreighoff, Morrice, Cullen and perhaps one or two others came and sang their song too early. Canada was still, to herself and to her painters, little more than an outpost of Europe. Other young painters of promise, returning from overseas to Montreal, found the country absorbed in Israels, Weissenbrucks, and the Maris family, and they migrated to the United States, or returned to Europe and spent most of their time there.

As it turned out, a Canadian art movement was started, not by professional painters, but by amateurs who fell in love with the spirit and scenery of our Ontario Northland. They went there to paint unequipped with the mental paraphernalia of academies and without any sense of the solemnity and importance of rules or methods, in pure holiday spirit; the business of art was subordinate to the joy of the adventure. This Canadian movement is distinctly a Canadian phenomenon, drawing its inspiration from the backwoods. The modern European schools have been largely influenced by Cezanne. The modern Canadian so-called school was inspired as the result of a direct contact with Nature herself.

CHAPTER I

The Beginning

THIS movement was started quite unconsciously by a group of young commercial artists employed at Grip Limited, designers and engravers, in Toronto, on some holiday sketching trips made to Northern Ontario. After months of commercial work in the art department, the stored-up creative energy poured out during the period of vacation.

In a sense it may be said that in Canada the amateur is honoured because the amateur attitude is democratic. It is the attitude of the great artist in all ages; the art critic with the professional bias, from the beginning until now, quarrels with the amateur's abandonment of professional methods.

In the group at Grip Limited, were Tom Thomson, J. E. H. MacDonald, Arthur Lismer, Frank Carmichael, Frank Johnston, F. Horsman Varley, Tom McLean, A. H. Robson, William Broadhead, Neil McKechnie and others whose names I have not been able to get. In Toronto half of the commercial artists were painters, while in Montreal painting and commercial art were two separate things. These Toronto men holidayed in the northlands of Ontario, where they sketched and felt at home.

Ontario has an area of which about five sixths is unsettled hinterland; a rough country of rivers, waterfalls, lakes, canyons, and great hills. The principal means of travelling when one leaves the railroad is by canoe and portage. The land has a peculiar magnetism. Once its air has filled your lungs and its spaciousness entered you, it calls you back. At night the stars look larger than elsewhere. In the daytime the sun is brighter. In autumn the colour is more vivid. In winter the snow is whiter. It is a dramatic land, sometimes stern, sometimes friendly. It lures you to learn what lies around the next bend of the river, over the ragged outline of a hill of spruce, or on the other end of a portage. Here is subject for art having new materials far from the ateliers of foreign lands, with "immutable essences" demanding of the artist more, much more, than a presentation of just the physical fact.

J. E. H. MacDonald was a sort of father to the tribe. As senior man in the art department at Grip Limited, and a workman with a highly developed sense of design, he became the one to whom the others were inclined to show their efforts.

MacDonald came to Canada from Durham, England, at the age of thirteen, but his father was a Canadian by birth, so that the son's line of tradition is here; indeed, his forbears were real pioneers. What little art training he had was obtained at schools in Hamilton and Toronto. He never received what in Europe would be considered the training of a painter. In 1911, just before we meet him, he had been elected a member of the Ontario Society of Artists, at whose exhibitions he had shown pictures. This organization, known as the O.S.A. was the only society of the kind in Canada that, in these early days, sought out and assisted young talent.

The English-born Canadian, with the Scotch name, painted pictures in 1910 that were silvery grey things of rivers and moonlit pines. Being a married man and not robust, he did not roam so far north as the others, but, as we shall see, the Ontario northland, especially the Georgian Bay, made an early impression on him. From 1908 to 1910 most of his sketching was done in the vicinity of Toronto, much of it snow scenes. In the O.S.A. show of 1910 he exhibited a picture described by a critic as having "a daring and rare vein of originality." This was written of a man whose originality, perhaps more than any of the others of the group which he afterwards joined, enticed the attacks of the critics for, with a brush in his hand and the autumn woods around him, he could let himself go in a manner inconsistent with his customary reserve.

Another of these Grip men was Tom Thomson whose name has become a sort of myth in the annals of Canadian art. Thomson's character was the antithesis of commercialism. He seems to have been a sort of modern coureur-de-bois. To-day a cairn stands on the borders of Canoe Lake, Algonquin Park, and on it is engraved in brass, "To the memory of Tom Thomson, artist, woodsman, and guide, who was drowned on Canoe Lake, July 8th, 1917. He lived humbly and passionately with the wild. It made him brother to all the untamed things of nature. It drew him apart and revealed itself wonderfully to him. It sent him out from the woods only to show his revaluations through his art, and it took him to itself at last."

Thomson was born in the village of Claremont, Ontario, August 5th, 1877. He had behind him a definite pioneer tradition, for it is said that his father drove with a horse, a democrat, and a spade from Claremont to Leith (near Owen Sound) looking for a farm and sampling the soil along the way by getting out of his democrat and spading over the earth until he found the ground on which he wished to settle.

Thomson, like MacDonald, was a natural artist

without academic training. As a youngster, a biographer writes, he lived the usual squirrel-hunting, apple-eating, cow-chasing, chore life of a farm boy. There is still a story around Leith that he once caused a mild commotion in the village church by drawing pictures in the hymn books. An illness in early life sent him to the woods which probably fixed his passion for northern nature. He tried to get the "hang" of business by a short commercial course in a business college, but it only made him less businesslike. When we meet him, he was a distinctive designer and letterer in the art department of Grip Limited. The main object of his later life seems to have been to stay in the woods and paint. When economic necessity drove him back to a desk, it was only for long enough to accumulate money to return north. Money meant nothing else. The having it on him was a nuisance. Once when some one had paid him for work with a cheque, he walked into the first bank on the street and presented it for payment. They asked for identification. It was an insult. Did they suspect that he was trying to obtain money under false pretences? He tore the cheque into little pieces, threw them in the teller's face and walked out of the bank.

A little money, helped out by fish and blueberries, went a long way in the north country. Occasionally, if funds were low, he became a guide to tourists. One of his excursions in this capacity seemed to amuse him when relating it afterwards. It was a party who let the guide do everything while they lolled around, smoked cigarettes, drank a little liquor, and felt superior. Thomson took them as far as he could the first day, doing all the paddling, portaging, and cooking, and finally put them to bed. He naively remarked later that when they woke up in the morning they had no guide.

This was Tom Thomson, impatient of swank, despising sophistication, and lacking the acquisitive instinct necessary to winning success in terms of the standard of his day; a bit of native genius that might have smothered out had it arrived in Canada earlier than it did.

A close friend of Thomson, and another of these Grip men, was Arthur Lismer, now vice-principal of the Ontario College of Art, Toronto.* He is a Canadian by adoption. His native background was the Yorkshire moors and stern English coast country full of big spaces and the mood of the sea. It was a good training ground for prentice hands, he says, which would some day tackle the hinterlands of Ontario.

Lismer went to work when he was twelve, and

*1925.

received his art education at an art school. Later on, with twenty odd pounds in his pocket, he went to Belgium for one year. About 1911 he came to Canada where he gravitated to Grip Limited. His early sketching here was done in company with Tom Thomson in the confines of Toronto. Each must have helped the other. Lismer's acute analytical faculty made him an invaluable critic, and Thomson's feeling for this country was of great use to Lismer. From the first he sensed the difference between Canadian and English landscape, the sharper outlines of the forms and the absence of atmosphere in Canadian landscape. He went off tramping alone, trying to analyze the problem of putting this difference on canvas. More will be said about this problem in another chapter, but it is interesting to remark in passing, that all of the artists of the group which he later joined, and who had painted abroad, speak of this difference.

Lismer, like the others, was a natural artist. His English parentage is incidental. He belongs here and was captured by the country's natural environment from the moment he set foot on these shores.

I have specifically mentioned MacDonald, Thomson, and Lismer because of the prominent part they play in the events covered in the succeeding chapters. F. H. Varley, Frank Carmichael and

Frank Johnston are others of whom more will be said presently. Enough has been indicated to show how genuinely an amateur movement this was. Here were a group of men answering to the conditions which we have insisted upon as being necessary in order to have a Canadian statement in painting; a group of men in love with the Canadian backwoods, donning the outfit of the bushwhacker and prospector in order to satisfy a need they felt to express themselves, and using their environment as a medium for this expression. Lismer says, speaking of their creative problem, "We felt locality but not mood. We felt topography but not colour. The fact was we could neither draw nor paint. We were adventurous, but it never got into our pictures."*

The following pages try to show how these problems were solved. The story is unique in the history of art. It is not, however, so much the story of an art movement as of the dawn of a consciousness of a national environment which to-day, is taking a most definite form in the life of the nation.

The industrial and commercial idea which is supposed to be the slayer of the arts, was, if possible, more heartily Canada's religion in 1910 than it is now. Just previous to 1914, Industrialism and Commercialism were looked upon as sort of twin

*Notes written for the author.

"Princes of Peace." It was widely believed that they had made war impossible. Their prestige in this respect was afterwards destroyed.

But opposition and friction are functionaries of the creative process. Poor men in their adversity create wealth for themselves and likewise men conscious of spiritual poverty search out and accumulate spiritual wealth. The spiritual famine which follows the triumphant advance of material progress will eventually cause us to re-plant our fields so that we may harvest food for our souls as well as for our bodies.

Canadian art budded from a civilization of iron and steel in Toronto, one of the chief industrial centres of the Dominion. What brought it to fruit was the law that accomplishes similar fruitages in all countries, in all ages.

> It is not from the sky;
> Flying not down from heaven, but storming up.
> Strange storming up from the dense under-earth
> Along the iron to the living steel
> In rose-hot tips, and flakes of rose-pale snow
> Setting supreme annunciation to the world.

CHAPTER II

Lawren Harris

LAWREN HARRIS was studying in Europe while the Grip group was breaking into the north country. Harris, like the others, was a natural artist, but his life had been different. He was born in Brantford, Ontario. The family had lived in this country for generations. On both his mother's and father's side was a pioneer tradition. The company with which his father was associated had pioneered in Manitoba and the Northwest in the days when the Canadian Pacific Railway was being built. His grandfathers had been pioneer Baptist ministers.

Harris's earliest environment was typical of the Canadian small town—swimming in the Grand River in summer, skating and hockey in the winter, and rubbing against types of all grades of society at the public school, a Canadian institution which would have been praised by Walt Whitman for its "levelling to divine averages."

In the course of a conventional education, we find Harris at Toronto University, filling his note-book with pencil sketches of his fellow freshmen and various members of the faculty instead of listening to professorial lectures. One of these illustrated notebooks was left by accident in the class-room where it was picked up by a professor intelligent enough to see that this student was wasting his time at college. He called at the family residence and stated his opinion, and the incident ended by Harris being sent to study painting in Germany.

He returned home in 1909, but almost at once left on a trip to Arabia to do illustrating for *Harper's Magazine*. The next years he was back in Canada, but went off again the same winter for Harper's to the lumber camps of northern Minnesota. The place he visited was one of the most primitive of its kind on the continent. He saw life as it is lived in the raw with women, bar-rooms and shanties. The lumberjacks were put to sleep with a shot of dope in their whisky and piled like cordwood in the shed after their pay had been extracted from their pockets. The experience finished off his education. After the studio life of Europe and the more contemplative east he dropped into a backwoods environment. By contrast, the impression must have been deep.

The years abroad so far as Harris's outlook and art are concerned have always been as if they were not. He forgot them the day he got home. His first exhibited work in Canada is the expression of an exuberance in his native surroundings; city streets, rows of houses and shacks in winter sun, snow and rain, behind brilliant autumn leaves. "These pictures," he says, "were painted in quite a different manner, technique, arrangement, and spirit from any work I had done before. I was far more at home in them than any place else and naturally forgot the indoor studio-learning of Europe, being simply dictated to by the environment and life I was born and brought up in!"*

These canvases of Harris's, when first exhibited at the O.S.A., were a new note in Canadian art, fresher, gayer, more natural than most of the others. There was none of the romance borrowed from the Barbizon school and nowhere in them a suggestion of European traditions. As he himself says, "they were the natural expression of a love for homely subjects with their roots firmly fixed in the every day life of all Canadians." The winter sun and snow and brilliant autumn leaves were appropriate symbols of Harris's own outlook. They have always deeply moved him. "Snow sheds an old familiar glory into one's rather foolish soul," I have heard him say. "There is so very much in whiteness."

---

*Notes written for the author.

LAWREN · HARRIS

Harris was exactly the type needed to give support and enthusiasm to a new art movement. He had private means. He believed whole-heartedly in the country, and was certain it had a spiritual contribution to make. The adoration of the Canadian Art authorities for old world art nettled him. He abhorred the tendency he saw around him to pay homage to the past. "It is blasphemy," he says, "to wilt under the weight of ages; to succumb to second hand living; to mumble old dead catch phrases; to praise far-off things and sneer at your neighbour's clumsiness." He hates repression. "The irrepressible," he writes, "creates ceaselessly fresh moulds for its future widening."*

Harris began to look for competitors to welcome. He must have felt a little strange among his old friends who belonged to the successful class and were not interested in art. He was not in on the game of empire-building and money-making and had no reason for joining it, so he rented a room for a studio over Giles's grocery store on Bloor street and started to create a world of his own in which to live and work. Presently we hear of him avariciously reading books on mysticism. His thought was coloured by the works of A. E., the Irish poet and mystic, with their plea for a national culture for Ireland. Much

Contrasts, by Lawren Harris, published 1922.

of what this writer says of Ireland applies aptly to Canada. "You can draw inspiration from other races," says A. E., "but their culture can never be a substitute for our own."† The exposition and enlargement of this theme in Harris's reading confirmed and expanded what his own intuitions told him. He began to round out a philosophy and a message with which to greet those competitors of his whom he hoped to meet.

He met them at the Toronto Arts and Letters Club, Old Court House, where several of the Grip men lunched. He says he was impressed with a private exhibition of sketches of Jim MacDonald's painted in the locality of the Humber River on the fringes of Toronto. I have never seen any of these, but I have seen others of the same period. They have not the exultant rhythm, the bold design and brilliant colour of MacDonald's more recent work, but they are an honest, unaffected expression of a nature full of natural poetry.

Harris induced MacDonald to leave Grip Limited and devote himself to serious painting. This had been a dream of MacDonald's for years and the infectious enthusiasm of his new friend made him consent. Harris was helped in his persuading by a friend, Doctor J. M. McCallum, who has been a

†*The Interpreters*—George Russell.

sort of godfather to the movement since its beginning.

The doctor owned a summer cottage on the Georgian Bay. He had sailed the Great Lakes in an open boat from Toronto to Michipicoten Harbour on the north shore of Lake Superior. He had been bitten by the North, a bite for which there is no cure. He had little interest in art from an academic standpoint, but he wanted to see a painter go up to the Georgian Bay country and put it on canvas the way he (the doctor) felt about it.

Harris told him of MacDonald. McCallum went to see the exhibition of his sketches, and was so impressed that he sent him up to his summer cottage, fitted him out with a house-boat and moored the MacDonald family in a channel off Split Rock Island, outside Go-Home Bay, twenty odd miles north of Penetanguishene. MacDonald went to work.

I have seen several of his sketches from this trip. Silvery blue lyrics they mostly are, a little tight. They impress one as being a natural expression of first contacts with immense spaces, such subjects as a commercial artist might be expected to choose who suddenly finds himself transplanted from a commercial art room to a peaceful seclusion with Nature at her best. There is the ever-present Georgian

Bay sky with its constant drama of dawns, clouds, and sunsets. There are the low-lying rounded shoals where the water curls into fascinating designs among the crevices and cluttered channels. To MacDonald, a passionate nature-lover, it must have been a cleansing experience.

In the fall Harris and his new friend went to the Laurentian Hills, north of Montreal, and came back with sketching materials out of which to build canvases. They tried to set down their own re-actions and to forget art rules which they felt hindered this natural expression. At the 1912 O.S.A. show Harris exhibited a Laurentian canvas "A Deserted Barn," which a critic described as "consummately ugly and compelling." MacDonald had "an early morning thing where a figure climbs over clean blue winter shadows, reeking with the nip of a healthy cold."*

I have no doubt too that the new friends had much to talk about up in the Laurentian hills. Their coming together had meant no less to one than to the other. Through MacDonald, Harris met the Grip group. They brought their enthusiasm for the north country, their love of adventure, their own peculiar outlook and their personal ambitions to paint. Thomson was still in the process of filling up before pouring himself out in his subsequent creative

*The quotations are from the *Canadian Courier,* 1912.

period. Lismer was trying to solve the problem of seeing Canadian landscape with Canadian eyes. Tom McLean was roaming the wilds of northern Ontario painting out-of-the-way nooks. He was one of the first to believe that it was a painters' country. Carmichael, the youngest of them, had left the trade of carriage painting to enter commercial designing and was saving his pennies to go to Europe and absorb an art education. J. W. Beatty on the other hand, who had been trained in Europe, was declaring that he had found enough material on the fringes of the Ontario northland to make him forget the old world for the rest of his days.†

They were a rebellious crew; rebellious toward all that was considered "the thing." Harris, perhaps the greatest rebel of the lot, was lit up with the conviction that Canadian painters had something worth while to say if they would only be themselves. A critic has said that Harris has in him "a streak of Heine and a streak of Whitman, and the two do not blend." He remains to this day an enigma to the reviewers, yet his position is clear. He has stated it himself.

"There are two ways of interesting oneself in art," he writes. "The first is a mere matter of satisfy-

†J. W. Beatty was not a Grip man, but he was a close friend of Thomson and the others.

ing the possessive instinct; of inflating the personality; . . . of looking always to other people, other times for all created works, and ignoring or decrying all native endeavour . . . In brief, it is the way of the plutocrat and incipient plutocrat to self-glorification. Of these we have had many."

"The second way is the way of life. This way demands an interest in what is being done to-day in our midst; the furthering of all original expression in one's own community. It requires a perspective that relates near and distant happenings and brings all findings to bear fruit here and now; and a vision that sees that never was anything created anywhere, at any time, save it was in defiance of all catch-cries, the now-heres and now-theres of the moment. It sees that life is creative, and that people only live when they create, and that all other activities should be a means to creation."

"It requires courage to face and to conquer the immense weight of inertia and the dead and dying traditions and sophistications that clutter the minds of men and mould them into the mimicry of living ways; . . . it requires a conviction that every people has a unique contribution to give to mankind, and that this they must make or remain sterile, subservient, sallow; and that this contribution they must have commenced to make before they can hope to understand the spirit that informs all great works and inspires all noble living."‡

Harris asked for the country what he asked for himself, namely, the freedom to express himself in his own way, and he was willing that "the proof of the poet shall be sternly deferred, till his country absorbs him as affectionately as he has absorbed it."

‡Harris, in *The Canadian Bookman.* An article on Sir Edmund Walker.

CHAPTER III

Signs of Revolt

THE first hint the public received that a movement was awaking in the country came at the 1912 exhibition of the O.S.A. in Toronto. Augustus Bridle was writing art criticisms in the *Canadian Courier,* and no better reviewer could have been found to give the advent of the new Canadian spirit a cordial reception. Never since has such genuine enthusiasm flowed with the ink from the critic's pen in Canada.

The stage for this exhibition was set beforehand by two unusually dull shows of the conventional type. A loan collection had opened the season where was displayed the opulence and taste of those individuals in the country considered by themselves and the public as the most important representatives of Canadian culture. As far as we can learn, there was not a single Canadian landscape. There were Dutch windmills, German forests, English duchesses, feudal castles, Venetian canals, and still-lives of fruit and old brass kettles;—nowhere a snake fence, a

Quebec steeple, a northern beaver dam, a touch of Canadian autumn, nor a whiff of the north. Canadian opulence bought pictures as it bought stocks, bonds, rugs, or antiques.

The exhibition which followed was a show by the Royal Canadian Academy. It seems to have been an echo of the one before it. Bridle says it was "a highly instructive and perfectly dignified collection of canvases possessing somewhat the same interest as might be excited in rummaging through a book of old prints with here and there a modern photograph. —But"—he exclaims,—It is not modern Canada. . . A visitor to this show would not be seized with the feeling that Canadian painters had got far beyond their tacit homage to the old masters who painted before Canada was discovered by the white men."*

Not until the spring of 1912, when the Ontario Society of Artists put on its annual exhibition, did there appear anything that told of the speeded national heart beat. The group at Grip Limited had come home from their vacations six months before with sketches of out-of-the-way places in the backwoods and several of them had pictures on exhibition. "Beatty," says Bridle, "who used to revel in Laren and Bruges and Paris,—Heaven be thanked that he has ultimately and almost completely turned

**Canadian Courier.*

his brush to depicting Canadian landscape, especially the north!"

Beatty at this time was one of the strongest advocates of a Canadian school of painting, but in later years less and less of his work has appeared, while the initial spontaneity has waned. Thomson was too busy roaming to care much for exhibitions. As yet the public did not know him. He had made trips northward with several of the others who were trying to paint the country. He knew it more intimately than any of them and had within him the potential equipment for its expression and a feeling for its design, mood, and colour, although he did not yet know how to lay the paint on canvas.

Lismer had been out on his own for weeks and was just beginning to see interpretative possibilities for the first time. He was a thinker of the same class as Harris, but as a black and white artist he had trained himself to look for outline. The entrance of colour into the composition raised problems, and in the north country he met with something entirely different in mood from anything heretofore encountered. The landscape was seen under a clearer atmosphere and in more elemental forms. There was a more rapid movement of light and shadow on the surfaces of these forms and the natural effects were not those which operate among verdant woodland or merely pastoral uplands. They were bigger and more epic in quality with larger rhythms which demanded bolder handling, and for this he was struggling.

Harris was showing his first collection of Canadian pictures referred to in the last chapter; canvases of city streets and rows of houses in winter sun, snow, and rain, behind brilliant autumn leaves. He had a scene from the land of the lumberjacks with pine-covered hills and some lumbermen driving a log boom down a river.† MacDonald attracted attention with a canvas entitled "Tracks and Traffic," which one reviewer (not friend Bridle) describes as "an ultra modern Whistler."

Let Bridle give us the atmosphere of this fortieth exhibition of the O.S.A. It is the first outbreak of the movement, the story of which we propose to tell; the first sign of an organized revolt from a too-long projected past.

"It must be admitted," writes Bridle, "that the old society (the O.S.A.) has taken a stride which bewilders the chronic damners or the casual newspaper critic, in many cases bored by the pictures. The man who could be bored with this show must be colour blind. I recall some shows of the O.S.A., to enter which was like going to hear a long sermon and

†This canvas was called "The Drive."

leaving with an indefinable tired feeling. Not so this one. There is an exhilaration, almost an abandon, that convinces any average beholder of the vitality of Canadian art which a few years ago showed signs of senility."

"There has been a house-cleaning. Here we have the first satisfying depicture of Canada, not merely of farm landscapes and pastorals and smug interiors, and pretty women and more or less smugly comfortable citizens; but Canada of the east and west,‡ north and south, of railways and traffic, and city streets; of types of people (though all too few of these) and phases of development."

"Of course, some artists allege that subject is of no importance; that technique and atmosphere and tone and highlights and juicy paint and superb texture and breezy handling and 'swish and go' and heaven knows what, are the things to look for in a show. But the same artists know right well that 'subject' to the average appreciator means half the battle; that to a Canadian, scenes in this country are of vastly more interest than all the fishing smacks and brass kettles and sea-weed sonatas of north Europe."

"So there are at least twenty of the exhibitors at

‡C. W. Jefferys, better known for his black and white work, was exhibiting some prairie canvases.

the O.S.A. who have translated the joy and savagery and crudity and peaceful picturesqueness of Canadian life, leaving those who prefer the melancholia to depict the sorrows."—

Oh, for more reviewers like Bridle! He has a lonely glory in the annals of Canadian art criticism.

"Let us hope for more of the same!" he cries—"This is modern and a note of great joy."

A joy, oh, Augustus, which too few of your countrymen know! The north is here—its incomparable sunlight; its whiffs of balsam, pine and spruce; frost-touched corners of the forest; the splash of tumbling rapids and cub water-falls. The land is beginning to talk. The studio windows are shuttered up and cobwebs hang on the slats. Something is being born. The tang of the north is colouring souls as it colours the leaves in autumn.

CHAPTER IV

A. Y. Jackson

IN Montreal, while Harris, MacDonald and the others were fanning the first flickers of fires in Toronto, another fire glimmered.

Montreal is an older city than Toronto, with more millionaires, older families and more claim to the prevailing ideas of culture, having been the chief trading place of Canada since the days when it was called Hochelaga. It is the vortex-centre of the industrial idea which permeates the land, a city where someone has estimated there is more Dutch art than in any other city of North America.

Why this vogue of Dutchmen? True, the windmills are picturesque and the canals have quaintness, but one of our snake fences, quite as picturesque in its way, called forth among the Montreal collectors nothing comparable in enthusiasm to that awakened by the windmills of Zyder-Zee and the dykes of Dutchmen. Of course there were notable exceptions like Sir William Van Horne whose judgment was as remarkable as his tastes were catholic. His collection ranges all the way from Rembrandt to Cezanne, includes Monets, Sisleys, Pissarros, one of the first El Grecos in existence, remarkable Goyas and other treasures. But in his attitude toward Canadian art generally there were no bold ventures like he made in other fields.

Here in this hive of industrialism, A. Y. Jackson was born in the year 1882. Before he was very old the family moved to a suburb of the city where, as Jackson writes, "there were plenty of kids to scrap and a country beyond filled with all kinds of wonder."

Nature got a chance at him young. His eldest brother was somewhat of a naturalist and together they collected everything, birds' eggs, insects, flowers and queer stones.

Jackson brought a love of the beautiful with him. Beauty lives lonely like a sleeping angel in the lap of the soul. At first only suspected or felt in little breath-blown stirrings, like long spears of grass in ever-so-little nibbles of a breeze. Yet that which is so gentle has power to drive a man through all but overpowering circumstances to an end which in the beginning, is only vagueness, but which clarifies like the dawn.

Jackson was intended for the insurance profession, but while waiting for an opening, went to work in the lithographing business. At odd moments between messages, he copied drawings, and while at this one day his employer set him to work in the art room where a specialty was made of designing labels for beer barrels and salmon and tomato cans. This was after leaving the public school at the age of twelve. At the end of six years he was earning six dollars a week.

But the drive had started. At the noon recess the artists in the drafting room would draw one another's portraits. When work was over for the day, Jackson rushed up to the Fraser Institute to read. On Saturdays he went sketching. Sundays it was church, Sunday school and more church. On holidays he and his eldest brother roamed the country on twenty-five or thirty mile hikes. They went to art exhibitions and admired all that Montreal had to offer. There was "The Stream in Autumn," by Gay, so wonderful you could count the dead leaves. There was "The Cavalier Chased by Wolves," the sort of subject the *hoi-poloi* liked. There were the Dutch pictures so preciously displayed in Scott's window. All marvelous paintings!

He left the lithographing business and started designing, reserving three days a week for sketching and hikes. This was made possible because of the greater skill and speed he had acquired in making a design.

One summer he and his brother signed up as hands on a cattle ship bound for London. They visited Paris and ambled north as far as Rotterdam, taking a curious look at the Dutchmen whose work was so admired at home. In Paris they met two Montreal artists, Clarence Gagnon and Boyd. They pored over pictures in the Louvre and other galleries in the city and by the time they returned to Canada, Jackson had determined to go back to Paris to study as a designer. With this in mind, he began banking his savings.

In 1906 he went to Chicago, attaching himself to a firm of commercial designers in the daytime and at night attending lectures at the Chicago Art Institute. It had a fine library and courses in composition, drawing and illustrating, and it gave to Jackson the first real training he had had in the fundamentals of his craft, but it was only a taste which whetted his hunger to study abroad.

So in the spring of 1907 he returned to Montreal and by working all summer, saved sufficient capital to go to France; fifteen hundred dollars it was, but one can live a long time on that in Paris.

His first six months were a hard grind at Juliens Academy. It was his initial experience as a real art student after living in a world of dull routine and commercial art. In Paris he found enthusiastic students from all parts of the world. The names of painters which stirred so much exuberance in Canada were there scarcely known. He accumulated a respect for the artist, *qua* artist, Michael Angelo, Leonardo da Vinci, Rembrandt, Sisley, Segantini. These were names to conjure with; these men stood at the forefront of mankind.

Jackson returned to Canada two years later (1909). He had decided to be a painter. He had been driven to a vision. (One never can rightly say whether we are driven or led.) The clear Canadian landscape stirred him, he says, more than the old country villages or Venetian canals. That winter he painted a canvas called "The Edge of the Maple Wood" and another, "The Old Barn." The first was to become one of significant interest to Canadian art.

In May, 1910, he first saw the Georgian Bay. "This land," I once heard him say, "Le Bon Dieu made on a holiday, out of sheer joy." The Georgian Bay is stripped of the ornamental trappings of the traditional forms of art expression. There is an austere serenity in the rounded rocky island forms expressive of a baffling but superb identity. The spirit in them is a distinctly detected "thing in itself."

A. · Y. · JACKSON

I do not think that Jackson was as deeply stirred by this country in 1910 as later. He did not know it yet. His visit was a flying one, for he soon had to return to Montreal, compelled by financial circumstances to re-enter the photo-engraving business, where he spent a miserable year drawing shoes and farm implements in the daytime and designing cigar labels at night in order to save money.

At this time in Montreal, so far as the artists were concerned, the time-honoured Dutch tradition in painting was definitely abandoned. J. W. Morrice was exerting an influence. His boldly summarized designs with Cullen's vigorous, stern, open-air work ended the Barbizon and Dutch domination. Clarence Gagnon was painting high-keyed landscape in a quieter mood. A. H. Robinson, an Ontario born artist, with something of the quality of Morrice painted along the docks and streets in gay colour and posterish design, but there was little encouragement for anything but foreign art.

There was no Bridle in Montreal to cry "This is modern and a note of great joy!" The press was indifferent or ignorantly opinionated and the more sensitive artists recalled the friendly associations of Paris. Morrice, as we know, finally left the country for good.

To this day the modern artists of Montreal have

kept in much closer touch with Europe than has the modern movement in Toronto. This has given the work of the Quebec painters a certain derivative quality. Most of them have drawn their inspiration chiefly from France. Toronto drew its inspiration from the backwoods. Hence in Montreal one may find a greater technical facility in handling paint. She was quicker to realize the importance of design and organization. Her artists were more familiar with the work of the French impressionists, a few samples of which drifted into the country, although in Canada in 1911 Cezanne, VanGogh and Gauguin were considered lunatics by the few who had seen them.

By the fall of 1911, Jackson had saved another thousand dollars and in September went off on a trip to Brittany, Etaples, Assisi and Venice. By that time his funds were exhausted and he returned to Montreal at the end of the following year. His tripping for the time was over and his next journey to Europe was as a private in the Canadian Infantry.

Here, then, was Jackson at thirty years of age, faced with the artist's old problem of an inner and an outer necessity. Was it coincidence that he returned home in the same hour that the new movement was beginning to make headway in Ontario?

CHAPTER V

Nineteen Hundred and Thirteen

FROM the time of the 1912 exhibition of the O.S.A. in Toronto, the new movement received momentum from many outside sources. A current passed through the country; a manœuvring of spiritual forces took place. Jackson and his friends were to feel the effect of it in Montreal, as we shall see.

In 1913 we read in the year-book of Canadian art published by the Toronto Arts and Letters Club that "our art will never hold a commanding position until we are stirred by big emotions born of our own landscape . . . and held to patient and persistent endeavour by the pioneer spirit which animated the explorers of early Canada."

This was a new note. It was emphasized by one of the older painters, a member of the Royal Canadian Academy. The younger men were to carry the idea forward. As has been said, all things were ready. The first sign that something was being born had been welcomed by Bridle as a note of great joy. Even in Ottawa, the seat of the Government, things were astir. Mr. Eric Brown, the new curator of the National Gallery, announced that "the time is ripe for Canada to have a national gallery worthy of its best traditions . . . to aid the development of Canada's art and her citizens' understanding of all art by every possible means, and to provide the necessary education for this development by the best exhibitions of the world's art obtainable."*

Another outward sign of the new spirit was the opening of the Ontario College of Art in Toronto under the auspices of the Ontario Government. It began its work in October, 1912, as the offspring of the old Central Ontario School of Art and Industrial Design, and its activities are becoming a leavening influence in the life of the entire province.

Still another sign was the announcement at this time that plans had been completed for the commencement of a building for a new art gallery. The Grange, the home of the wife of the late Professor Goldwin Smith till her death, was bequeathed to him while he lived, and at his death to be given as an Art Museum. The City of Toronto bought additional land adjoining the Smith residence and agreed to contribute a grant toward the upkeep of the property. The Ontario College of Art was to have its

**Year Book of Canadian Art,* 1913—Toronto Arts and Letters Club.

quarters in the same group of buildings. Thus the Dominion Government, the Government of Ontario and the City of Toronto all went on record as being interested in the development of the creative life of the country.

But perhaps of more direct importance to the artists who were launching the new movement, was the appointment of the late Sir Edmund Walker.† president of the Canadian Bank of Commerce to a directorship of the Canadian National Gallery at Ottawa, as well as to the presidency of the Art Museum of Toronto. Sir Edmund seems to have been the only business man of wide influence in Canada who was conscious of the forces which were shaping events at this period which Harris has called "The dawn of a spiritual consciousness in our people." He alone, of all the men of affairs in the Dominion, showed a personal human interest in the painters. He alone seemed to see the necessity for creative expression in the building of nationhood and publicly declared it. His presence therefore at the National Gallery and the Grange was an encouraging thing to the movement.

And what of the actors in the play? The painters themselves?

†Then Mr. Byron E. Walker.

The Grip fraternity was breaking up. Lismer returned home on a visit to England in 1912. Robson moved to another establishment and Thomson, after a summer in the north, followed him. Carmichael went to Belgium to study art.

Tom Thomson had started to paint. In 1912 he had been on a canoe trip to the Mississauga country with one, Bill Broadhead, a Yorkshireman who worked at Grips. About 1910 the Mississauga Forest Reserve was set aside by the Ontario Government as a reserve for game and timber. It lies north of the Georgian Bay and is most conveniently entered by canoe from Biscotasing, a lumbering town on the main line of the Canadian Pacific Railway, ninety miles west of Sudbury. The Mississauga River ends in a forty-mile rapid, finally emptying into the Georgian Bay at Thessalon. The timber rights have now been leased and the forest is making its last stand. It was considered a long way north in those days; the sort of country Thomson loved, with twisting rivers, broad blue lakes and many rapids.

On his trip to Mississauga, Tom produced about twenty small sketches, low in tone and laboured; just shore-lines and old swamps; mist on lakes and smoky dawns; moods smudged into panels. "But they were awakenings," says his friend, Lismer, "and we all saw that fall when he came back, that not only was Tom opening up as a painter, but that the northland was a painters' country."‡

This was a more important discovery than it now seems. Just as Kreighoff, the German, nearly fifty years before had come to Quebec and seen in the French habitant new and picturesque art material, so in Northern Ontario these painters found new and picturesque landscape, typically expressive of the Canadian spirit. The discovery was to give direction to Canadian art. It was to dictate its mood, technique and method—who can say for how long!

It is hard to see what outside events influenced Thomson in these early days. Lismer, who was with him a good deal, thinks that MacDonald, in his quiet way, had much to do in coaxing out the genius which afterwards flowered, "although," says Lismer, "we learnt as much from Tom as he did from us." Another influence was Doctor McCallum. It was through MacDonald that the doctor met Tom. "The door opened and in walked a tall, slim, clean-shaven, dark chap who was introduced to me as Tom Thomson," says McCallum.* Later, the doctor went out to hunt him up. He knew the name of his street and rang the door-bells until he found the house.

‡Notes written for the author.

*Article in the *Canadian Magazine*.

Thomson was out. McCallum climbed to his room in the attic and waited. Some sketches were lying on a table and when at last the painter of them came in, he found the doctor interested. "Take them home with you," said Tom, "They're no good."

McCallum took them home but returned them later. He had found the man whom he thought could paint his north country to suit him. Thomson was taken up to the Georgian Bay cottage on Monument Channel and from then on McCallum kept him under his wing. He bought, or helped him to sell sketches, went north with him frequently, and saw that he was never in want for the necessities of life.

Tom painted a canvas he called "Northern Lake" and exhibited it at the 1913 spring exhibition of the O.S.A. beside the works of his friends. It was his first exhibited canvas. A reviewer describes it as "a rolling composition of waves and rough weather with a distant shoreline." Northern Lake is now in the Normal School at Ottawa. It was bought by the Ontario Government the year it was shown for a price of $250, a fortune it must have looked to its painter.

This 1913 exhibition of the O.S.A. was like a repetition of the one in 1912, when for the first time Canada invaded a Canadian art gallery. A reviewer, like Bridle, friendly to the movement, comments upon it in the *Year Book of Canadian Art,* 1913. "Harris," he says, "paints the usual thing, the commonplace (a corner store this time) with a zest that no study in Germany could give him." MacDonald, true to his feeling for the decorative is now "rolling his cloud-forms over stern, rocky ridges of the north, or boldly facing the summer glare of the Lakeland." Lismer showed "The Clearing," painted at York Mills, near Toronto, a characteristic piece of farmland fringed with woods. This canvas of Lismer's and Thomson's "Northern Lake" were later bought by the Ontario Government.

In the fall of 1912 an exhibition of Scandinavian art was held in Buffalo and thither went MacDonald and Harris. Sweden, Norway and Denmark with an environment resembling ours have developed a national art of their own. Our painters might have learned something from the Scandinavians, but there were no examples in this country. The story of the rise of the Scandinavian native school of painting sounds like an echo of the story of our own. Christian Thiis, in his introduction to the catalogue of the Buffalo exhibition of Scandinavian art in 1913 wrote that the painters whose work was being shown "do not speak, do not attempt to speak that studio Volapuk; that facile salon esperanto which is so utterly devoid of character or vitality." Of Norway he writes, "Norwegian art owes little or nothing to the past."

It sounds like home. "There," says Thiis, "the public was quite at a loss for a clear understanding of this new open-air movement in landscape. The lack of a critic with a right understanding of the issues at stake widened and deepened the gulf that separated the public from the painter." Canadian critics in the main have been equally unintuitive.

At the exhibition in Buffalo, MacDonald was much moved by a canvas of Gustav A. F. Fjaestad, entitled "Ripples." It possessed (I judge only from a reproduction) a fine rhythm and striking design which appealed strongly to MacDonald. I have heard Harris say that a canvas by the Norwegian painter Schlberg, "Mountains, a Winter Landscape," was one of those which most impressed him. We can understand why, even from the print in the catalogue. The background is a high white form of snowy mountains, beneath a lone star, suggestive of a grand mood of life, an overtone of natural form which is a "thing in itself." The picture has a touch of what Harris so often tries for in certain of his own northern canvases.

Neither Harris nor MacDonald had as yet closed with the north as they did later. Subconsciously, however, they must have realized that they would enter it. Here was another artist trying to express the same north in another part of the world and the Canadian painters were afterwards accused at home of doing work derivative of these Scandinavians.

All of these exhibitions, appointments, and sales of canvases which came like streaks of morning light in 1912-13, made an impression on Harris. Fergus Kyle of the Toronto *Globe,* with whom Harris had been on sketching trips, wrote an article which expressed his friend's sentiments. "The time is ripening," wrote Kyle, "when the Canadian characteristic can be appreciated by the Canadian mind and can be put into pictures by Canadian painters at the same time having an appeal beyond the Canadian connoisseurs."*

But Harris did not stop at painting. He saw the vision of Whitman.

> What do you see, Walt Whitman?
>
> . . . . .
>
> I see the shaded part on one side where the sleepers are sleeping; and the sunlit part on the other side.

"Look ahead," says Harris, "disrespectful of Time's ways." He foresees the rise of a great native

***Year Book of Canadian Art* published by Toronto Arts and Letters Club, 1913.

literature of drama, poetry, philosophy and fiction. Pictures as a rule are the earlier forms of expression. Painting awakens awareness to natural environment; from this spring the other arts.

He determined to build a studio that would be a workshop for artists doing distinctly Canadian work. Attached to it he planned a little theatre, a combination of a picture gallery and a playhouse where young Canadian playwriters and painters were to be invited to send their work. The war which came in 1914 and the erection of Hart House theatre prevented the full carrying out of this programme.

Doctor McCallum agreed to help with the financing. The most pressing need was the studio, a workshop for the painters. This was to go up first. Rents were to be charged to cover the cost of maintenance, but no profit was thought of.

A site was chosen on Severn Street for a three storey brick building with a fine north light. McCallum agreed to share three-thirteenths of the cost and Harris contributed the remainder. It was to be called "The Studio Building for Canadian Art," a name to which some have objected as being too limited in scope.

Of all the projects undertaken or planned during this year of 1913 in Canada, the studio building was to have the most far-reaching immediate effect on

Canadian art. Here the new movement's activities eventually centred. By means of it, Jackson came to live and work in Toronto and those who were lukewarm like Thomson were pursuaded to paint.

CHAPTER VI

In Montreal

WHILE the modern movement launched itself with cheers in Toronto, in Montreal it was attacked. It was pointed out in an earlier chapter that, in the eastern city, the artists drew their inspiration largely from France, but in Toronto the incentive was the backwoods. Among the Montreal moderns were R. S. Hewton, who had returned from Europe with Jackson at the end of 1912, after five years study on the continent; J. G. Lyman and Mrs. Andrew Allan were each of them in sympathy with the modern movement abroad and their work when it appeared at exhibitions "plugged holes in the Dutchman" as Jackson put it, the Dutchman, as we have said, representing the prevailing art taste of the connoisseurs and critics.

But in spite of the influence of the Montreal press, which despised anything modern and favoured the Dutch and Barbizon schools, it was the modern movement that steadily gained ground.

A noble and sympathetic figure in Montreal through all these years was the late William Brymner, president of the Royal Canadian Academy and for many years instructor at the Montreal Art Association. He was steeped in the Barbizon tradition and was probably more of an authority on that period than any man in Canada. But while his students plunged into impresssionism, he neither lost interest nor sympathy, and had it not been for his fearless attitude, it would hardly have been possible to have exhibited modern work in Montreal.

The first important art event of the 1913 season in Montreal was a private exhibition held by Jackson and Hewton in the art gallery, to stage which had cost almost their last cent. Not a line appeared in the press about it. Scarcely a person came near it. Hearing that two members of the board of the National Gallery were purchasing canvases for the Ottawa collection, Hewton and Jackson sent them invitations to attend this show. Neither appeared. They confined their purchases to several canvases of deceased foreign painters, whose names even in ten years have been forgotten. "I wouldn't have minded if they had spent their change on living nonentities," said Jackson, "so long as some poor fool of an artist, Swiss, German or Irish got the money. But it all went to dealers. It would have been better to send an order over to London every year for three thousand dollars' worth of well-assorted."

Hewton and Jackson's exhibition was a complete failure. There was nothing to do but close it up and retire to the country where they could live cheaply. This they did, going in March to the town of Emileville, Quebec, to join the farmers in their sugaring-off season.

In the same month, the Montreal Art Association held its annual spring exhibition. According to Mr. Morgan Powell, art critic of the Montreal *Star,* this show marked a distinct departure from the old traditions. There were the Hewtons, the Jacksons, the Allans and the Lymans "plugging holes in the Dutchman." It evoked anger. The press was deeply stirred. It was suggested that if Montreal would join hands with London they might stamp out Cezanne and his neurotic influences.

Jackson seems to differ with the critics in his opinion of this show. "Have just been to the annual spring exhibition," he writes in a letter that year, "and my heart is heavy within me. Lessons in what to avoid howling at you in impotence; Nature by the yard copied in every way possible. The painting is right enough, but no one has anything to say; vain repetitions. Two Morrices and one Cullen, a couple of water-colours by Hugh Jones and one by Brymner was all I discovered to-day."

Jackson and his friends at this time had not the

defence that they were painting Canada in a new way. Most of their exhibited canvases were done while in Europe. But they were vigorous paintings, the artist's own concept of his subject, not a Dutchman's or a Frenchman's.

The Montreal *Witness* came out with a three line double column heading,—"Post impressionists shock Local Art Lovers at the Spring Exhibition.—Screaming colours and Weird Drawing Cause Much Derisive Comment—Younger Men Taking the Lead." Hewton is picked out as being "particularly staggering." He heaps on paint "by the spadeful." Jackson is given a close second for a canvas called "Assissi From the Plain."—"The emotion depicted," says the *Witness,* "is past finding out. Another picture of his, 'The Fountain,' shows that he can paint and paint well when he does not try to shock." John Lyman's "weird creations" included the portrait of a woman that "would disgrace a common sign painter" and the colour "decidedly raw." So the article goes on for two columns.

S. Morgan Powell of the Montreal *Star* was still more incensed. Starting with one of J. W. Morrice's, he goes through the list thoroughly, then expands his criticism beyond the immediate artists represented and attacks the whole impressionist movement in painting.

Mr. Powell took their followers so seriously that he delivered a lecture to the Women's Art Association about it. "Hard on the impressionists' heels," he told them, had followed "that coterie of poseurs, frauds, and sensationalists, known as the post-impressionists, with their formless daubs and meaningless arrays of graceless shapes." Canada has not wholly escaped. The walls of the art gallery (the half-million-dollar one) has been desecrated on more than one occasion by such daubs. The speaker used some striking imagery. "How could one consider deliberate ugliness as a form of beauty? As well argue that the scent of a skunk rivalled that of the lily because the oil of the former was used as a basis of perfume."

After all, one wonders what Mr. Powell really thought. Writing that same year about the same exhibition in the *Year Book of Canadian Art,* published in Toronto, he appears to hold quite another view. "There has arisen here (in Montreal)," he says, "a group of young, gifted and courageous painters who have ideas and the sense to use them; technique and pluck to experiment with it; talent and the knowledge that was not given them to be suppressed by any regard for convention. . . The younger men who have added emphasis to the note of departure are A. Y. Jackson, R. S. Hewton (and others). All show pictures that reveal originality, a striving to get away from the dull routine of convention that has meant so many dull exhibitions. Such works as 'Assissi From the Plain' and 'The Fountain' stamp A. Y. Jackson as an earnest student, a skilful draftsman, a colourist who is likely to make a name for himself and an artist of acute perception."

The article in the Montreal *Star* was not, however, allowed to pass unchallenged. Mr. H. Mortimer Lamb, a mining engineer now living in Vancouver, sent the critic-lecturer of the *Star* a lamb-like epistle in which he stoutly defended the Jacksons, the Hewtons and the Lymans, likewise Cezanne, VanGogh and Gauguin. He desired to remark on what he was disposed to believe were the ignorant comments of the critic. Since the time of Rembrandt the fallibility of contemporary judgment had been notorious. The critic preferred Delaroche to Delacroix. He damned Millet, ridiculed Manet and tried to hound Whistler. But history has proven him (the critic) to be a fatuous fool. Even the best equipped of critics can but approach such a task with fear and trembling.

One of the victims of the show had been J. W. Morrice. Lamb thought that Morrice is so big a man that no foolish comment of the sort can affect the high esteem in which he is held. The critic's references only irritated those who love and appreciate Morrice's very exquisite art.

The attack on the younger men is described as a cruel and ignorant one, which might well have serious consequences. Very few people in Montreal had yet seriously studied the modern art movement. The opinion of a presumably reputable writer in a reputable paper might, and very likely would, carry weight with the uninformed. These young artists were dependent on their art for a livelihood. At best, art affords a precarious living to those who forsake everything for its demands. The critic had been responsible for making the path so much the harder for young and struggling men who by reason of their undoubted talents are deserving of all the encouragement and support that we can give them. The critic, Mr. Lamb says, "belittles what he cannot understand, hates with bitterest loathing any suspicion of originality and bows down in worship to the obvious."

Behold then, another layman supporter of the cause! Lo, three had thus far stepped forward in this country of over seven million of souls; a doctor and a banker in Toronto, and a mining engineer in Montreal.

Jackson wrote bitterly of this spring exhibition

some time later in a letter to Harris. "After all the hooting is over," he said, "to sit down and read of VanGogh, Cezanne or Gauguin makes you think of the empty nonsense written by and about eminent British painters in the old-time popular magazines, and thoughts on art by old ladies without the necessary thinking apparatus. So-and-so tells how he came to paint his first picture and why he took to art. The honourable somebody else is asked who he thinks is the prettiest woman in art,—which is all taken seriously while these poor devils VanGogh, Cezanne and Gauguin put their heart into a movement which they knew would bring them no recognition during their life time. Their letters alone prove them to have had more intelligence in their little fingers than some of the others in the whole family. Anyway, not being endowed with the knowledge of a newspaper critic, I'll refrain from throwing mud until I know more."

CHAPTER VII

Jackson and Harris

WHILE these art issues were being fought out in Montreal, Jackson and Hewton remained at Emileville. It was the maple sugar season; the month of March; the time of year when in eastern Canada an occasional day brings a whiff of spring that coaxes one to go off to the woods. To Jackson, who had been roaming for four years, the impulse to be moving was strong, but this year he was tied by his financial circumstances. He had spent the most of his small supply of capital in that spring exhibition of his and Hewton's, which had proven a dead loss. The immediate future was uncertain. Recent events in Montreal had disgusted him and he thought seriously of migrating to New York.*

In the midst of his depression, he received a letter from J. E. H. MacDonald of Toronto. In 1910 Jackson had seen a small winter landscape of Mac-

*One canvas painted by Jackson on this trip had an interesting history. He was going to apply the paint remover and scrape it off in disgust when Hewton offered him a clean canvas in exchange. Ten years later the picture which escaped death won the Jesse Dow prize and was purchased by the Canadian National Gallery at Ottawa.

Donald's on exhibition in Montreal, which, he states, was the first Canadian canvas that awoke anything in him. "I was inclined to write Macdonald and tell him," he says. "The canvas showed little knowledge of continental works. It was a more direct reaction from Nature. It was hard and meticulous and lacked all the technical qualities of good painting, but there was a native flavour to it."

It now turned out that MacDonald had been similarly moved by a canvas of Jackson's, "The Edge of the Maple Wood," exhibited in Toronto three years before. The letter received at Emileville was to say how much it had been appreciated and to inquire if it were still unsold. MacDonald's letter stated that a Toronto artist named Lawren Harris wished to buy it.

To buy it!—Jackson must have read those three words several times. Who in Canada would want to buy one of his pictures? Who was this man Harris? What on earth was all this that MacDonald said about a group in Toronto and their aspirations for a Canadian art? They were putting up a studio building! Harris was writing him all about it. Harris thought Jackson's "Edge of the Maple Wood" the freshest, brightest, most vital Canadian note in the exhibition!

"The Edge of the Maple Wood" now owned by

Lawren Harris was painted in 1909, and is about the only Jackson canvas left of this period. He had just returned from two years study in Paris when he painted it, and, as we have said, the clear Canadian landscape moved him more than the old country villages or Venetian canals. Lismer describes the picture as "carefully drawn and significantly Canadian though somewhat sombre."† All the rising young group in Toronto seem to have recognized in it a definite break with tradition. Tom Thomson afterwards said that it first opened his eyes to the possibilities of Canadian landscape. It is rather quiet looking to-day; an honest statement, as Lismer says "rather sombre," without many liberties being taken with nature.

And Harris wanted to buy it! Outside of a few sketches of Venetian canals it was the first money that Jackson had been offered for his paintings, and it came at a time when it was badly needed. He wrote MacDonald that the canvas was still for sale.

By return mail came an effervescing letter from Harris himself, enclosing a cheque. The writer said they were getting a real Canadian art movement under way in Toronto. It had all started with a crowd of commercial artists going to Northern Ontario;—getting away from the old stuff into some-

†Notes to the author.

thing with a real native flavour;—some of them had quit the commercial game entirely and were spending all their time painting; they needed a place to work and were going to erect a studio building for Canadian art; Canadians ought to go quarrying in their own country instead of making trails all over Europe;—there was much to paint here but nobody up to the present seemed to have noticed it;—Jackson might ship "The Edge of the Maple Wood" any time.

On March 26th, 1913, Jackson sat down and wrote Harris the following letter in reply.

"It seems impossible for me to express myself in writing to you and Signor MacDonald without hunting up a new crop of words. Your letter arrived here last night with the cheque all safe. MacDonald tells me you are a real enthusiast, a good live artist; one who can practise and preach and wallop the Dutchmen when occasion calls, and judging by your letter, I strongly suspect that MacDonald is right. Those poor Dutchmen! If they were not already dead I would shed a few tears for them.

"It really looks as though the sacred fires were going to burst into flame in Toronto by the faithful efforts of yourself and MacDonald and the modest millionaire.‡ We once had some smouldering fires

‡Harris had mentioned Sir Edmund Walker as being interested in the new movement.

in Montreal which might have blazed up if they hadn't fanned them with bricks and wet blankets and built walls of pot-boilers about, cutting off the air and light. But when they built a new half-million-dollar gallery to house the crumbs and leavings of Europe, the poor fires petered out and died. Sad, isn't it?

"Yes, I am quite in accord with you. You have only to look over the catalogues of our exhibitions and you will see trails crawling all over Europe; 'Winter in Holland'—'Spring in Belgium'—'Summer in Versailles'—and 'Autumn on the Riviera'—Ye Gods!—Monet pottering around Jamaica; Picasso hard at it in Japan; Renoir out in the Canadian Rockies; Sisley in Sicily—and the French impressionists would never have existed.

"At the same time we must realize the limitations imposed upon the home article surrounded by people to whom art means nothing more than to go and copy something. Make something perfectly natural, fool people if possible, paint a stable and glue bits of straw on the front so you can't tell just when the painted article ends and the real stuff begins.

"I expect to go to Kitchener, Ontario, in about six weeks and will have an opportunity of meeting you. Studios! Modest millionaires!!—It all seems like a dream. So scared I'll wake up. Many thanks for the cheque. I'll put on two coats of paint now."

Jackson had made up his mind. Harris's cheque was the last short mile that separated him from commercial designing. When that was spent he had decided to go to New York where he hoped to save enough money in six months to spend the rest of the year painting. He was not going to desert altogether. It was Canada he wanted to paint. If ever anyone felt Canadian landscape, it is Jackson. His idea was to make a living in New York and paint here. In the last ten years he has painted the country from Halifax to Prince Rupert.

In May we find him writing again to Harris in a brighter humour. "Always glad to hear from you. It keeps me from getting petrified and scares away the germs of conventional academism. Still in the country with Hewton messing away with lots of paint, trying to make it interpret Nature without imitating too carefully. Everything is green now but the sky, which isn't any colour at all. It's so lovely and sunny and smells like spring, and sounds and feels like it, but to find the equivalent in colour for sounds, smells and other sensations is a problem which our strong, sincere old contemporaries have passed on to us. The Lamb and the Montreal *Star* had another round very violent on our side and quite conclusive on the other. I am enclosing a dear old grandmotherly article from the Montreal *Standard,* full of good advice to young artists. I feel pretty much as you do about American painting, healthy and vigorous much of it, and much of it slick and clever, but none of it profound. Still, I feel that we have a lot to learn from their out-of-door painters. The way they lay into a big canvas excites my admiration and yet it is decidedly limited. Expect to be in Toronto in a couple of weeks. I will be in Kitchener for some time and if you are not there will take a run over to Toronto when you return."

Jackson's comments on American art of that day give a hint of what was occurring in his own outlook. He realized that an out-of-door school of painting in Canada was inevitable and that the country would have to be painted on a scale proportionate to its spaciousness and spirit. An extract from another of these letters to Harris amplifies his point of view.

"Up to the present I have not done anything exciting in the country," he writes. "And yet it is there waiting. As you say, most of our work lacks feeling—plenty of sentiment and enough ability, but loftiness of conception is felt by its absence. I have decided to hit harder and I think I am succeeding, though no doubt losing other qualities in the effort."

Jackson like Harris, exchanged his overseas inspiration for the inspiration of the backwoods within a year after settling down to paint in Canada. The Georgian Bay, which he was about to visit, tipped the scale for him. Perhaps in no district in Ontario, unless it be the north shore of Lake Superior, is one more conscious of a mood. The Indians called it the Land of the Great Spirit and gave the name of Manitoulin (Isle of Manitou) to the island that lies across its northern coast for a distance of eighty miles.

From north to south, the Georgian Bay stretches a length of one hundred and thirty miles, with an average width of fifty hanging on the side of Lake Huron. It has a back-broken shoreline shivered into an archipelago of rocky islands scraped bare ages ago by the glaciers whose claw marks are still on the rocks, making rhythms of lines and patterns which change with the shifting shadows. Crooked windblown pines are on the islands. Their limbs twist away from the prevailing west wind and wave like black banners against unbroken stretches of pure sky. In stormy weather the trees bend before the wind, the whole shoreline appearing to crouch. One can sail a dingy up the coast from Nottawasaga Bay to Manitoulin, keeping nearly all the way in the narrow shoally channels, but the thing that stays in the memory are the vast open stretches of water. Early in the morning or on still days specks of islands in the distance seem to sit on air, their base separated from the water. At dawn or sunset anything may happen. One's eyes may picnic on colour or witness the austere storm signals of marshalled gold-rimmed clouds. On quiet evenings the bare, rounded rocks seem like the backs of whales above the surface of the water. They have an epic quality that is both kindly and austere. Man has not blasted them for minerals for the country is not of much economic importance now that the big timber is removed. The Georgian Bay is a playground in summer and the shoreline a sheet of ice during the winter across which the settler may drive his dogs or his horses *en route* for mail and supplies.

With the money which Jackson received for the "Edge of the Maple Wood" he went to the Georgian Bay, stopping off at Toronto where he met MacDonald. Harris was away. On his return, hearing that the Montreal man was visiting relatives in Kitchener, he went to see him.

There was lots to talk about. Harris was filled with plans for his new studio building and urged the other to come and live in Toronto in the new quarters for Canadian art. The building was to be finished by the spring of 1914. Then they could do something. The National Gallery was beginning to take notice and it was only a question of time before the public would realize what was happening.

So Harris talked, bringing to bear all his natural optimism and enthusiasm. Jackson was deliberate in his decisions and was never stampeded, but this fellow Harris had the same invigorating effect on the constitution as the nip of the season's first cold snap. Jackson took to the idea. Toronto might be possible if work could be found, otherwise it was out of the question. He had to make a living one way or another. Oh well, the autumn was still three months off. No use in planning that far ahead. He promised to look Harris up in the fall. They would see what turn things took by that time.

In August he went to Penetang and camped out all summer sketching and fishing, later spending a few weeks with some friends in the neighbourhood of Freddy Channel. When the summer cottagers had returned to the city, he set himself up in an old boat house and stayed on alone on Portage Island.

Portage Island is several miles south of Monument Channel where Doctor McCallum had his summer cottage. The doctor was getting ready to close up his place for the season when a letter reached him from Harris. "There is a Montreal artist named Jackson sketching somewhere around your part of the Georgian Bay," it said, "one of the younger crowd from Montreal who feels the same about the country as we do. I think he intends to stay late. We want to get him to come to Toronto and work in the new studio building, but he's hard up and talks about going to New York. If you see him, have a talk with him about it."

On the way up the doctor found Harris's friend at Cognashene, where he learned of his place of residence on Portage Island in Freddy Channel not far from Whalens. McCallum called in on his downward trip. It was turning cold and Jackson's shack was made for summer use. He was starting to cover the holes with birchbark and moss but the project was never realized for the doctor suggested that Jackson move up to the McCallum cottage at Go-Home Bay where there were no holes in the boards, plenty of firewood, canoes, rowboats, and a beautiful country to paint. A launch would bring Jackson down to Penetang when he was ready to go. He was welcome to stay as long as he liked.

At McCallum's he lived alone until the end of October. He saw the colour rise to its peak and the trees beginning to strip. The snow came setting patterns on the rocks, deepening the shades of the water and whitening the edges of the sky.

It is worth seeing, the Georgian Bay country in October, as autumn sings her glorious annual swan song. From McCallum's cottage you can row out to Split Rock and a harvest waits to be reaped by a painter like Jackson. Or you can "mosey" up Monument Channel where the Huron Indians made their last stand against the oncoming Iroquois, and get into a net-work of channels and bays until you reach the bay of Go-Home, so called because it was the route which the Indians took back to their home in the Muskoka country by way of the Muskosh River. If you want to follow their trail you turn to the left out of Go-Home, paddle a mile or two, portage your canoe and camp the night at Flat Rock Falls. From there you follow the Muskosh to Muskoka.

October crowns the cliffs maroon, crimson and gold. The poplars spark. The maples blaze in scarlet-orange puffs or deep reds. The oaks are glowing coals. The moss is bronze. The rocks turn mauve and purple, white and blue.

> The pines and spruces shake their heads and sigh
> As one by one the brown leaves drop and die.

Jackson painted a number of canvases. One of these he called "Land of the Leaning Pine," which catches an autumn gale when, as I have said, the whole shoreline of the bay seems to crouch and the crooked trees lean the same direction as the waves.

The canvas was bought by the Canadian Government six years later for the National Gallery. Two other works of this fall, "Blueberry Country" and "First Snow" are now owned by Doctor McCallum.

The doctor and Jackson became close friends. They talked things over. The younger man told of his plan of going to New York. His funds were exhausted.

Oh, that Doctor! He and Harris had fixed it all up between them I am sure. He knew how to get what he wanted. Jackson was induced to come to Toronto for a year and share Harris's studio until the new building was completed. The doctor guaranteed that pictures enough would be sold to meet expenses.

And that settled it.

CHAPTER VIII

Thomson Starts to Paint

THE year 1914 started auspiciously for our gathered group of painters. The studio building was completed that spring. The new movement had a home and the National Gallery was beginning to pay some attention to it. Fourteen Canadian canvases were added to the national collection. The press spoke of the three thousand, two hundred and seventy dollars spent on Canadian art by the trustees of the National Gallery as though it were a large sum. This was only because in former years so little had been distributed in this way. The amount would hardly have purchased one foreign canvas.

The skeptical critic and the collectors did not yet believe that an art movement could arise in Canada. "We have no atmosphere," was the common saying of those who regarded the still over-rated Dutch school of landscape painting as the culmination of all art. In both the public and private collections of the day, Canadian pictures were largely ignored unless they were of the most conventional type.

Ideas as to method, though still hazy, were clarifying. With most of the new group the decorative quality was strongly marked. We see this particularly emphasized in the work of Harris who, at this time, was doing a number of decorative snow scenes with the use of plenty of paint. As yet there were not many of the north. It was in them that he eventually found himself.

But this decorative quality in Canadian art was something new. The exponents of conventional art, as we have said, insisted on atmosphere, which pleased the collector. Art, however, has a higher function than to hang on the fringes of society. This group had ideas and ideals. Here was landscape material for art which the old methods failed to interpret. They saw nothing in the popular forms of art which struck the note they all felt here. New methods had to be created. The feeling grew that the misty landscapes of the French and English schools copied widely in Canada were out of character with Canadian jack-pines, burnt-over hills and the rough and rugged north. Artists were afraid to paint clear and sharp what they undoubtedly saw clear and sharp. As long as mists and hazes were introduced the clear-cut forms of the north country lacked vigour and conviction. Art must take the road.

THOMSON · STARTS · TO · PAINT

It was after coming to Toronto that Jackson painted a large Georgian Bay canvas nick-named by the others "Mount Ararat." It had faults and was not exhibited till several years later, but it was swung in a new direction. MacDonald did another "Laurentian Hills" which, like Jackson's, had a fresh twist. Design and colour were made more definite while atmosphere was left to take care of itself. These features of bold design and colour became a mark of the group's work and more attention was given to modelling and depth in form, thus getting away from purely decorative design.

Thomson, as yet, was not an initiated member of the fold. On coming to Toronto, Jackson met him for the first time. The two took shares in a studio at the new headquarters. Jackson, with his Julien training, at once saw the possibilities of his new friend and realized also his limitations. He says of Thomson's work that at this time it was interesting but tight and altogether photographic. He did not realize that he possessed a large store of knowledge which he was not using for he had a distinguished sense of colour and was an excellent designer, but before Nature he took no liberties.

Tom's most difficult stumbling block was a disbelief in himself. He had fits of unreasonable despondency. He was erratic and sensitive. Harris tells how Thomson would sit in disgust for half an hour before a freshly painted picture flicking matches at it until the wet paint was covered with them.

In the studio with Jackson this backwoodsman learned how canvases are built up. He was sincere and had a marvellous knowledge of nature with a passion for colour. His sense of design, which Jackson speaks of, had been developed under MacDonald at Grips. His work grew bolder, simpler, more glowing and original in colour. His form-sense ripened. Astonishing advancement was made. The others encouraged him all they could. Harris visited the studio daily praising everything good, bad and indifferent. Lismer, who shared a shack for a season with Thomson at the rear of the studio, gave his friend the benefit of his keenly analytical criticism, and while all helped Tom, they each were helped in turn by him.

In the meantime, Jackson was passing through the ordeal of criticism and experiencing for the first time the Toronto brand of abuse. Shortly after coming to the city he was elected a member of the Toronto Arts and Letters Club where, at the suggestion of his friends, he exhibited some of his Georgian Bay sketches. Enough has been said as to the direction of his work at this time to suggest the character of these pictures. They were totally unlike the conventional thing, broad in treatment and accentuated in design and colour.

It was a bomb to H. F. Gadsby, a writer on the Toronto *Star,* who after seeing them at the club, returned to his office and wrote three columns headed "The Hot Mush School." What began as pure fun degenerated into ridicule of an extremely ignorant variety. Gadsby pictured himself and his friend Peter Donovan, another newspaper man to whom "all intellectual movements were as welcome as a cold in the head," trying to understand this new school of painting.

"What is this picture, Peter?" asks a bystander.

"That," says Peter, "is a plesiosaurus in a fit as depicted by industrious and misguided Japanese who scorn foreground or middle distance."

"What do you make of this one, Peter?"

"It looks to me like a Dutch hedge cheese having a quarrel with a chunk of French nouget, but I suppose it is called 'Moonlight in Jerusalem.' ". . . So it went on for two columns.*

It looked like what it was,—a noble wind-swept country of twisted pines, blue water and rocky forms that held aloft splashes of autumn colour like grandmother's old patch quilt. That was what the eye

**Toronto Daily Star,* December 12th, 1913.

saw. What neither Gadsby's eye nor his newspaper man's nose for news could discover was the gesture of the painter attempting to set down his honest re-action to rhythms and forms in Canadian landscape, subordinating and simplifying detail to design in order to express his joyously felt mood.

For the first time a Canadian newspaper critic was attacking, not an individual painter, but a cause. MacDonald and his friends prepared a reply outdoing Gadsby in his Gadsbyisms and saying no more in two columns of newspaper space than his opponent. Nevertheless it was a reply and from this time forward these men became the champions of their own cause.

The winter wore on and Thomson hungered again for the north. Jackson must see Algonquin Park, "his country" as Tom called it, and Harris backed him up. Thomson had work to do so his friend Jackson, after worming a promise from him to follow, in February departed northward. "It is just as Lawren said," he writes in a letter to MacDonald, "You don't notice the cold a bit. All you notice is your breath dropping down and splintering on the scintillating ground. At Canoe Lake Station it was forty-five below last night."

"Had a little five mile workout this afternoon. The weather was milder and not at all penetrating.

It was sunny, but not colourful. The woods look very wonderful and full of decorative motives; deer trails all over the place, and wolf trails too. I think if I have a scrap with a whole pack and get eaten up it will be a great add for the studio building."

He adds as a postscript, "It appears that Tom Thomson is some fisherman, quite noted around here."

Algonquin Park is twelve hours' journey by train north of Toronto. Almost all of Thomson's canvases and sketches, the latter aggregating about five hundred in number, were done here. The group as a whole has hunted other fields since the park became civilized and a place of boys' camps and summer resorts. The country in winter presents beautiful decorative compositions. Harris hardly ever failed to paint the spruces after a snow storm, their boughs drooping with fresh white blobs.

Jackson remained in the Park for a couple of months being joined for a time by J. W. Beatty and J. E. H. MacDonald, after which he and Beatty went to the Rocky Mountains. Thomson arrived as the last snow left and was joined shortly by Lismer. The black flies drove them out by the end of May, but only for a time. In August, Thomson was back after two months' visit with Doctor McCallum on the Georgian Bay.

It seems that at last, after years of observing the things of the north, Thomson was finding himself. The short three years' period of his creative achievement which culminated in his death, began in the fall of 1913.

When Jackson returned from the Rockies, he found Thomson alone on Canoe Lake. Tom was rapidly gaining in power. The photographic fidelity of his earlier work was giving way to bold summarization. His colour had a remarkable sombre richness and a feeling of great solidarity which commercially trained painters usually lack.

Tom himself was aware of what was taking place. Jackson says he was as happy as a child if a sketch turned out well and discouraged to the point of throwing away his paint box, sketches and all, into the bush when something eluded him.

But the year which started with so much promise for the little group ended under a cloud. On August 4th, 1914, war broke out with Germany and from that time on Jackson became restless. When he and Tom returned to Toronto in the autumn the recruiting sergeants were on every down-town corner. The group met at the studio and each produced his summer's work. All overflowed with enthusiasm and a joy which few outsiders perhaps appreciated when they saw Tom's harvest.

Whitman writes, "The American bard shall be noted for generosity and affection and for the encouragement of competitors." This spirit has always been the mark of this group of painters. Had it not been so, a nature as sensitive as Thomson's could never have produced its best work. Thomson and his genius might have lived together a life-time in the same body without the world knowing them. The impression has spread abroad that Thomson himself was the founder of the Group which afterwards received the name "The Group of Seven." It will be seen that this is incorrect. His work was an inspiration to them all, but it is not depreciating him in any way to say that he himself was a product of the movement, owing perhaps more to it than any other single member.

CHAPTER IX

Entrenched

WHEN war was declared with Germany in 1914, the new movement was entrenched. Morgan Powell, the art critic of the Montreal *Star* had launched a preliminary attack on what he called the impressionistic Canadian school in the spring of 1913. H. F. Gadsby in Toronto had caused another skirmish in the early months of the following year. In each of these instances, Jackson had born the brunt of the onslaught while the others were left alone. What had been written in the press about their work had, in the main been favourable but during the four years of the war there was a lining up of sides in the field of Canadian art. A number of other painters, besides those specifically mentioned here, were painting Canadian landscape in a Canadian way, but Harris, Jackson, MacDonald and Lismer became the most radical and militant. These men had dug themselves in and on almost every occasion, when as a group they exhibited, the press struck hard.

This was because the break with Europe and conventions became more definite and pronounced. The critics did not realize that they were fighting not a group but an idea, and because the artists painted from a conviction within themselves, while their opponents could make no appeal except to conventions, the new idea gained ground.

In March, 1915, the O.S.A. held its usual annual exhibition, the first since the clan had gathered. All of them sent and had canvases accepted, built up from the year's sketches. Jackson had "A Winter Afternoon"; MacDonald, "Snowbound"; Harris, "Winter Twilight"; Carmichael, who was back home and to whom we shall refer presently, was exhibiting his first accepted canvas, "Winter Evening"; Lismer's was "Sunlight and Shadow", and Thomson's, "Northern River."

It was an important moment. Thomson was expected to make something of a sensation. Every one of the canvases, while not radical compared with present day standards, represented a definite departure from the schools.

More than they might have hoped for happened. Thomson's "Northern River" was called "the most striking canvas in the gallery." An article in the *Christian Science Monitor* of Boston written by a Toronto correspondent described it as a picture "in which is given a virile rendering of the tangled confusion of the fringe of the forest, the still surface of a river, the serrated purple silhouette of woods in the middle distance and a salient curve of the river bank, touched with the ruddy glow of the setting sun." The writer commented on the flare of colour and the presence of North in the gallery. "It revels," he says, "in what the rest of the world might consider the country's defects. Those predominating features of Canadian landscape, rocks, pines and snow, find many champions among the painters and the Canadian adds the aphorism that a landscape is not beautiful in proportion as it is reminiscent of Europe."

One Toronto paper took upon itself the duty of giving these young men a friendly sermon. "There are times," it said, "when in the present exhibition the progressives seem to over-reach themselves. In music the use of shock and discordance has become with some of the futurists, mere affectation. They undertake to see significance in almost anything that departs sufficiently far from the accepted canons of composition. Among the newer artists, there is something of this assertion of the right to do just as they please, based on the assumption that the layman is an ignoramus and the objector a pedant. There is a modern notion that the man who creates in any form of art has only to say that he is doing things the way he feels and sees them and that he then stands justified. This is an important truth exaggerated to an illogical conclusion and may lead to the painting of magenta snow and sea-green flesh tints."

We suspect that the magenta snow was Jackson's whose insistence on painting the mantle of the north under shadows of mauves and blues has, to this day, baffled the honest critic who sees only whiteness. Alas for the artist who perceives colours that others miss and has the courage to paint them! Jackson himself, in his struggles to simplify his compositions, still murmurs that he cannot in honesty make a shadow have one colour.

The view that these artists were banking on the ignorance of their public or covering up a lack of draftsmanship with the explanation that the public did not understand art, is a criticism which has been made of modern painters by newspaper writers in nearly all countries, a view which is common to the man in the street, because it is flattering to his judgment. Enough, I think, has been told of the lives of these Canadian painters to establish at least their honesty of purpose and their ability to draw.

It was about this time that Canadian artists, under the sponsorship of the Royal Canadian Academy, started a travelling exhibition of pictures to raise war funds. The members of the group joined other Canadian painters in sending canvases without charge, and the newspapers, which found it so hard to speak or believe enthusiastically in Canadian art, wrote laudatory articles to induce the public to buy on this occasion. I have at hand a clipping from one Toronto paper pointing out to its readers that the object of the exhibit was not a mere appreciation of artistic merit, but that the Royal Canadian Academy might be able to hand over to the Patriotic Fund the sum of $16,000. The outcome was that the Patriotic Fund received $10,514 by these unusual promotion methods while during the period of the exhibit's travels from coast to coast an aged artist in Montreal died of starvation because he refused to accept money from charity.

The war made its first definite impression in Canada early in 1915 after the first battle of Ypres, where many Canadian soldiers were among the casualties. The original belief that all would be settled in a few months gave place to the realization that it was to be a long struggle. One could feel its shadow deepening. Jackson was beginning to have visions of voyages far afield. It came close to Harris when his brother enlisted for active service in France. It came close to all when it was seen that work even of the commercial type was difficult to sell, while the engraving houses and advertising agencies, the last line of retreat for these men in the struggle for existence, were diminishing their art departments and jobs were scarce.

A few days before Christmas, 1914, Jackson went back to Montreal. The year was over during which Doctor McCallum had guaranteed a living from Jackson's art if he would make his home in Toronto. The war had made him restless. His friends in Montreal were enlisting. The issue of the struggle from his angle of vision was becoming clarified to his own discomfort. Moreover, it must be remembered that he had spent three of the happiest years of his life in France and she meant more to him than to the others. The combination of these influences were slowly creeping in like a tide.

For a time we find him again at work in Emileville where several canvases were painted out of doors. One of these "Maples in Early Spring" was bought by the City of Sarnia, Ontario, about 1920.

But the war fever was reaching a crisis. Jackson's friend, Hewton, had signed up as a private with the 24th battalion. Jackson himself, found it difficult to sustain his own interest in painting. After the first battle of Ypres he enlisted with the sixtieth battalion of Montreal, joining up in June.

The new school of painters in the vernacular of those war days had dug themselves in. Their numbers were lessened by one with the departure of

Jackson. His place was taken by a younger man, Frank Carmichael, whom we have mentioned before. The necessity of supporting a household has hindered Carmichael from taking the place in the movement which he might have. His life story is one containing the same elements of struggle as Jackson's and Lismer's.

Carmichael was the son of a carriage maker in Orillia, Ontario, which is on the borderland of Northern Ontario, so that this man had been familiar with the northern mood from birth. He had a craving to paint pictures and in 1911, when his father sold out the carriage business, we find Frank at Grip Limited as a junior, when Lismer had been there less than a week. The Orillia boy arrived in Toronto with the sum of thirty-five dollars in his pocket, receiving as wages $2.50 a week. In the fall of 1912 he and Thomson moved over to the firm of Rous and Mann and were joined by Varley of whom we shall hear more presently.

Carmichael, like so many other Canadian artists, had a hankering to get to Europe. Lismer and Varley, when they came to Grips, told him of the Academie de Beaux Arts in Belgium, where it was possible to attend art classes and receive tuition free. The idea of getting to this Academy became a purpose which was objectified in September, 1913, when, having scraped together $350 by saving $10 a week of his $15 salary, he left for Europe.

Day and night for nine months he worked at the academy, sometimes sketching out of doors in the afternoons. For three more months he worked in England, until his financial resources became exhausted and during all this interval he states not a single sketch was painted which, to his way of thinking, showed any promise.

In the following year he was back in Canada. At home, on New Year's Day, 1915, while sketching out of doors in a temperature of twenty below zero, for the first time a composition went together to suit him. A similar sort of experience is cited by Lismer, who tells how it happened that one day alone, while painting on the Credit River, he suddenly succeeded in bringing through what he felt.

Carmichael was in a seventh heaven. His adventure in art had brought him to the same discovery which others of the group had made, the discovery that Canadian landscape with its baffling spread of shadow and clear atmosphere could not be handled in paint by the same methods as those successfully employed in the more vaporous atmosphere of the older art countries. On his return to Toronto a new bond had been made between his old friends Lismer, Harris, Thomson and MacDonald.

CHAPTER X

MacDonald's "Tangled Garden"

"OH, where, oh where are the Jacksons, the Allans, the Hewtons and the Lymans who used to disgrace these walls" asked an elated Montreal critic in reviewing an exhibition in Montreal some time in 1916. Once more the walls of the art gallery were hung with mild and inoffensive pictures. The moderns had gone.

Jackson received a copy of the paper while in the line near Ypres and wrote the Editor:

> DEAR SIR:
>
> "While holding down a small section of the line in Flanders, I became aware that some poor fish was sniping me from the rear. Now as to 'Where, Oh Where!'
>
> "Mrs. Allan is with the Red Cross in London. Hewton is recovering from trench fever somewhere. Lyman is working in a hospital in Estaples, and only strategic reasons prevent me from telling you precisely where private Jackson is."

But in Toronto art was on the move, though Harris had signed up and was training at Camp Borden, and Lismer had gone to Halifax to paint for the Canadian War Records and take charge of the art school in that city. In the summer of 1915 Lismer had obtained a position as instructor at the summer school of the Ontario College of Art which led later to an appointment in Halifax. In Halifax we leave him for a little time, while he paints pictures of the hulls of camouflaged transports.

The first appearance of the group's work at the exhibition of the O.S.A. in 1915 caused, as we have seen, mildly adverse comment. In the following year they succeeded in creating something of a sensation through a canvas, strange to say, of the meek and mild MacDonald.

Perhaps it was that MacDonald's good academic reputation gave cause for the greater animosity at the alleged burst of radicalism which marked the appearance of his famous canvas "The Tangled Garden" shown in that year. Whatever the cause, this picture received more publicity in the newspapers and more strongly impressed the work of the group on the minds of the Toronto public than any other which had yet appeared. From this time forth, for the next three years, MacDonald was looked upon as the most radical member of the group and an exchange of invective and retort followed which was both humorous and bitter.

"Tangled Garden," even to-day, is a striking canvas of a garden in late summer when all the entourage of brilliantly coated bloom nods from a perennial border in dazzling summer glory. MacDonald painted what he felt of rhythm, colour and decorative pattern submerging detailed representation perhaps more severely than it had yet been done by any Canadian artist. As a piece of design, it is an achievement. In the gallery under the lights it resembled a strip of tapestry done frankly for the decorative motive and showing a pronounced interest in design. It was astonishingly unconventional, but possessed no small amount of enthusiasm and feeling for riotous tangles of colour. It does not look so radical to-day as it did in 1916.

The critics attacked this canvas as a robin seizes a worm. It shocked, angered and disgusted their esthetic beliefs for it pressed one to think of art in different terms than the Canadian critic had yet accepted. The painter's joy in doing such a creation called for a response to something beyond the honest critic's personal experience.

A reviewer in the Toronto Daily *Star* wrote of the new school's examples at the 1916 O.S.A. show, —"There are some samples of that rough, splashy, meaningless, blatant, plastering and massing of unpleasant colours which seems to be a necessary evil in all Canadian art exhibitions now-a-days. It is quite unnecessary to particularize them. Nobody visiting the exhibition is likely to miss having his or her sense of colour, composition, proportion and good taste violently affronted by some of these canvases; some large and some small but all tinged with the same blustering spirit of post-impressionism; all conveying the same impression that the artist was out to make a sensation, didn't know how to do it and wasted considerable good pigment in a disastrous attempt."

Hector Charlesworth in *"Saturday Night"* held to the view that a picture ought to be more than a shout; it should be something with which a man might comfortably live, and something truly interpretive. "Oscar Wilde has stated" said Mr. Charlesworth, "that Nature constantly imitates art. If this be true and Canadian Nature essays to imitate some of the landscape to be seen at the O.S.A. exhibition, then we shall all have to wear smoked glasses."

Mr. Charlesworth has retained his dislike for this new school of painting to the present time. When it received its first favourable recognition at the British Empire National Exhibition at Wembley in 1924, he had the courage to ruminate in melancholy fashion that England should think the paintings of these men representative of Canadian art and Canadian landscape.

But it must not be supposed that the "Tangled Garden" drew upon itself the full indignation of the press. MacDonald had two other canvases in this exhibition, "Elements" and "Rock and Maple," either of which according to Mr. Charlesworth might just as well have been called "A Hungarian Goulash" or "Drunkard's Stomach," beside which the critic thought "Tangled Garden" a masterpiece. Charlesworth speaks of the group's work as a whole as "being inspired by no sincere passion for beauty hidden or revealed, but savouring of the ideal of the vaudeville manager whose motto is 'Hit 'em in the eye.' "

But that Mr. MacDonald is a gifted man who can do something worth while, i.e., something Mr. Charlesworth liked, is shown in his canvas "Laurentian Village, October" which is well composed and rich and subdued in colour. Mr. Frank Carmichael, a promising young man who will do good work when he finds himself, is represented by three large landscapes which seem to show the seeking after strength to which allusion has been made (in speaking of MacDonald), and the same may be said of a picture of Arthur Lismer's, although "A West Wind,

Georgian Bay" has fine atmospheric qualities. Mr. Lawren Harris sends a fine snowscape which is one of the best pictures he has painted since adopting his present style. It is finely composed and has qualities of depth suggested by the hills in the background which is admirable. Among other artists represented meritoriously is A. Y. Jackson.

This, in effect, is Mr. Charlesworth's summary of the work of the new group as represented in 1916. He omitted to mention Thomson's "Birches" and "The Hard Woods," described by another critic as being marked for a fondness for intense yellows, orange, a strong blue and altogether a fearless use of violet which can scarcely be called pleasing, and yet which seems an exaggeration of a truthful feeling that time will temper.

The truth was that the work of the new school had the critics in confusion. That anything in the nature of an important art movement should be rising here in Canada was more than they could credit. They held the view of the average Canadian and could not be drawn into the pretence of liking what was an outrage to their esthetic sensibilities. Art and its influences were vague, far-off eventualities which must come with a prosperous, populous civilization. We should advance gently and stick to conventional subjects for the time being. Mr. Charlesworth prefered such canvases as "Near Tower Bridge" a London scene which he describes as "meticulously and charmingly painted"; or "The Decline of Day" in which the drawing of ships is excellent; or a very charming and interesting " A Curtain Call" which is one of those theatrical decorative pieces "warm, yet delicate in colour."

MacDonald was informed that his "Tangled Garden" was too large for the canvas; that the colours were crude; that it was not allied to anything known as art. So hopelessly at sea were the comments that he forsook his usual suave calmness and prepared an article on "Canadian art and Tangled Garden" in particular for the columns of the press. From this time forward these painters knew that they could look for little if any constructive or intelligent criticism from the newspapers and that they must follow their own gleam or be overwhelmed by a weight of ignorant misapprehension which, if allowed to impinge deeply, would drive them to imitative mediocrity.

So in March 1916 MacDonald sent his article to the Toronto *Globe*. It was printed under a box heading on the editorial page with the title "Bouquets from a Tangled Garden" and preserved in print as a record for those of posterity who wish to read it.

"It is probable," says MacDonald, "that artists

generally are glad of the publicity given them. Their work is made to be seen and although they would prefer to note more frequently in their critics an intelligence at least equal to that expended by themselves in their painting, and would naturally rather become noted than notorious, they like to hear the big guns of criticism whether directed against them or fired in their favour. It is evident that a drive of some kind is on. That is better than stagnation in the trenches."

Describing the criticism of the show as a gas attack, MacDonald speaks of the remarks of the critics as literary, sententious, eloquent and paternal. "They are learned in the law, know something of Ruskin, Whistler, Benjamin West and Oscar Wilde, but they seem to have derived little from their study beyond the power to quote precedents for their action. . . One would think that if it is the function of the artist to see, the first duty of the critic is to understand what the artist saw. Yet they condemn apparently without understanding and without making an effort to understand, forgetful of Gœthe's caution for doubtful cases, that 'a genuine work of art usually displeases at first sight, as it suggests a deficiency in the spectator.' "

"One makes no claim that the 'Tangled Garden' and other pictures abusively condemned by the critics are genuine works of art, merely because of their effect upon them, but critics may be assured that they were honestly and sincerely produced. Their makers know when vaudeville ideals are in keeping. If they planned a hit anywhere it was in the heart of understanding. They expect Canadian critics to know the distinctive character of their own country and to approve, at least, of any effort by an artist to communicate his own knowledge to that character." . . . "One may assure the critics that it can be demonstrated that everyone of these pictures is sound in composition. Their colour is good, in some cases superlatively good; not one of them is too large. Their nationality is unmistakable. Undoubtedly they are not what the artists would like them to be, but they are truly interpretative if one understands and is interested in Canadian landscape. . . It would seem to be a fact that in a new country like ours, which is practically unexplored artistically, courageous experiment is not only legitimate but vital to the development of a living Canadian art."

" 'Tangled Garden,' 'Elements' and a host more are but items in a big idea, the spirit of our native land. The artists hope to keep on striving to enlarge their own conception of that spirit. And they remember sometimes that the best in this kind are but shadows, and the worst are no worse, if imagination amend them!"

CHAPTER XI

Death of Thomson

THE purchase of one or two of Thomson's pictures by the National Gallery and odd words of appreciation from some of the more discerning of the critics, helped to inspire him with the confidence in himself he needed. The enthusiasm and affection of his associates and the feeling that he was living for a cause strengthened his desire to work harder. He was aware of what was happening in himself and was stimulated to attempt one large canvas after another. Although there was never an artist who thought less of the returns he might receive for his work, he was wise enough to know that before a widespread spiritual movement can be achieved a people must work *with* its artists for to work *with* them is to work *for* them.

When Tom was pursuaded by his friends to make his city quarters at the studio building in Toronto, an old cabinet maker's shop, originally part of the property, had to be fixed up like a northern shack. Harris had it lined with beaver board and knocked a window through for an east painting light. Here Thomson lived, cooking his own meals and sleeping in blankets as he was accustomed to do up north. Lismer shared this place with him during the winter of 1915 and 1916. When Tom was not painting, he amused himself by making fishing trolls with piano wire and colored beads. He never quit thinking of the woods. Their rhythm was in his soul.

Although this man was a painter, he was more. The poetry in Thomson's painting ranges from superb lyricism to the lyrically epic. For a dozen or more years he had lived in his north country being much alone, often spending the night in his drifting canoe. There are sketches of his done before dawn from the middle of a lake, and several of his pictures were painted at night in the heart of the bush. It was the only place he felt at home. When the ice broke on the rivers in the spring, he left for the North and remained there until the winter froze him out. In the city he scarcely ever showed himself on the street, but at night he would put on his snowshoes and tramp into the country.

Tom was again in Algonquin Park in 1916. His creative period, the short moment of productiveness during which his entire life seems to have found expression, was at its peak. A technique entirely his own appeared and the cries of the wild were in every stroke of his brush. Anyone who has seen his "Jack Pine" or "West Wind" or "The First Snow Ducks" or any of his successful canvases of this period cannot fail to recognize the work of a great artist. His colour is sombre and deep. He summarizes a complex subject, like a tangle of branches and underbrush, with the assurance of a master. In his pictures there are poetry, joy, the reach of spaces, the pageant of the northern autumn, the drama of the sky and swirl of waters in the wind. There is that sweet loneliness which is exaltation.

He painted intuitively surrendering to the mood of his environment. Lismer says "When the rest of us were slaving to harmonize the contrast of some autumn colour-composition I have seen Tom leisurely open his sketch box and allowing himself to go with the stream catch in a few moments the spirit of the scene without being at any time conscious of our problems."

He knew the woods as the red indian knew them before him; the strange night cries of the birds and untamed beasts that frighten the timid stranger; the hardly-perceptible twist of the twigs which indicate the direction of the prevailing winds. He knew the craft of the woodsman and was acquainted with the turning order of the colour as the autumn foliage crisped and fell. He knew the time of the flight of the first wild duck and the time of its return in the spring.

Never before had such knowledge and the feeling for such things been given expression in paint. Thomson's canvases are unique in the annals of all art especially when it is remembered that he was untrained as a painter. His master was Nature. He learned to use the knowledge gained as a professional designer for the purpose of creative expression and his extraordinary range of palette was developed during the last three years of his life.

In Thomson we have the poetry of a new part of the earth, new that is to art. What an experience it is to go through a pile of his sketches on little panels iced over with thick pigment, for he used paint lusciously. It transports you to ranges of the open air never before transfused to canvas, vibrating with light which would have driven the French impressionists mad. He leads one into cool gnome-like spots where wool-white water spills into miniature canyons; or to a trout stream in moonlight with flecks of silver beams on the leaping rapids; or again, you have nosed a canoe into a snaggy shore of drowned spruce and balsams and catch a glimpse of a sluggish northern river coiling slumberously between spikes of stripped black-purple trees; or again you come to a country of clean scaly rocks with heroic, clinging little pines and watch the wind make speckled frolic on a scampering lake. Dawns, sunsets, vibrant days, grey days, moonlight, sunlight, twilight, midnight, all as they are in the north are lovingly but never sentimentally painted by Tom Thomson. There is no trace of an intellectual philosophy, nor of a theory of esthetics; no preachment on life, no effort to impress or improve, or lift you up, or cast you down, but just pure "being" as though northern nature itself were speaking to you through a perfectly attuned and seasoned medium. The west wind blows directly in your face without any artistic obstructions; the scent of pines and balsam and wet mosses; the spray of falling waters, the cold effulgence of snow, or the nip of late fall when the wild geese fly, is around you as you look at Thomson's pictures. Each stroke is clean and deliberate and full of meaning. He repeats forms and rhythms intuitively and his designs are spacious and loftily composed. The sombre deep tones set all in a minor key. Never do we find a light or flippant touch. Some of them are amazingly daring and all-unconsciously bold. In the foreground of his "West Wind" canvas is the trunk of a pine tree which he paints in a certain kind of red, organic to the design, but in all probability entirely unlike the original. Jackson said it was the same sort of stroke as

William Blake made when he wrote "Tiger tiger burning bright". One knows that actually tigers do not burn, but what does that matter? It is perfect and satisfying and thrilling to the imagination like Thomson's tree.

This picture has in it the same spirit of reverence as the religious paintings of the old masters. What they felt for their madonnas Thomson re-experienced in his contact with northern nature. "West Wind" has a fullness and richness of colour, a power and sureness of execution rarely equalled in paint. There is the dignity of a great symphonic march in the succession of oncoming waves. One sees the water in the middle distance between two pines, one bent to a bow like the side of a harp. On the other side of the lake, still hills calmly blocked against a moving sky seem stiffening to the breeze. It is northern nature poetry which could not have been created anywhere else in the world but in Canada.†

His "Jack Pine" is a devotional meditative study. A single tree stands spreading the tracery of its limbs and branches like the pulsating veins of Mother Nature. Behind is the jack pine's native background, a northern lake with its dark undulous-creeping shores. One could believe that this tree was to the nature-worshipper Thomson what the

†"West Wind" is now the property of the Toronto Art Gallery.

symbol of the cross was to a mediæval mystic. And not only his jack pine has Thomson exalted, the pulsating vibrations of light are reverently painted in hundreds of little brush strokes, not sharply and lightly pointed as Monet paints, but soberly and with loving pressure.

"First Snow Ducks"* is in another mood. The magic of late fall has turned the northern landscape of Algonquin Park to a cold blue with a white rim on the horizon of the sky. The autumn colour has ripened to acorn browns and the outlines of the hills are sharp and severe with a remote quality about them. Here and there on ledges and crevices and sunken places, a patch of snow sparkles in sunlight or loses its sheen under heavy scrolls of clouds. This particular canvas is one of the simplest of Thomson's compositions. A strip of shivering water laps past in the foreground rimmed by a piece of straight shoreline in the middle distance which rises to low rounded but sharply defined slopes. Most of the picture is a reach of leadened sky and high up over the lake is a flying phalanx of ducks. Without detail Thomson gives us in simple dots of paint the moving poise of a flock of birds on the wing, that movement which in the flight of the wild ducks is so imbued with intelligent instinct, so articulate of a

*"First Snow Ducks" is now owned by the City of Sarnia, Ontario.

directly moving life-force in Nature. Thomson himself felt this force and moved with it in the last three years of his life. His snow ducks, like his jack pine and west wind are neither philosophy nor painting in the studio sense, but pure poetic expressions of the feelings and sensations of a nature worshipper's soul.

Thomson's pictures recall a passage in Whitman's Preface to Leaves of Grass in 1855, a document which every Canadian poet, painter and critic may read and re-read without in a lifetime of work exhausting its directions.

"The art of art, the glory of expression is simplicity," writes Whitman. "Nothing is better than simplicity,—nothing can make up for excess, or for the lack of definiteness. To carry on the heave of impulse and pierce intellectual depths and give to all subjects their articulations, are powers neither common nor very uncommon. But to speak with the perfect rectitude and insouciance of the movements of animals, and the unimpeachableness of the sentiment of trees in the woods and grass by the roadside, is a flawless triumph of art. If you have looked on him who has achieved it, you have looked on one of the masters of the artists of all nations and times. You shall not contemplate the flight of the gray gull over the bay, or the mettlesome action of the blood horse, or the tall leaning of the sunflowers on their stocks, or the appearance of the sun journeying through heaven, or the appearance of the moon afterward, with any more satisfaction than you shall contemplate him. The great poet has less a marked style, and is more the channel of thoughts and things without increase or diminuation, and is the free channel of himself. He swears to his art 'I will not be meddlesome, I will not have in my writing any elegance, or effect, or originality, to hang in the way between me and the rest like curtains. I will have nothing hang in the way, not the richest curtains. . . What I experience or portray shall go from my composition without a shred of my composition. You will stand by my side and look in the mirror with me.' "

Thomson's death occurred on Canoe Lake, Algonquin Park, July 8th, 1917, where he had been painting since early spring. The park warden at Mowat Lodge, a mile or so away found an upturned canoe and that is all we shall ever really know of the end. Jackson heard it at a camp in England where he was waiting, after being wounded, to receive his lieutenant's commission. Varley was also overseas. Lismer had had a letter from Tom not long before which reached him in Halifax where he was painting official pictures of camouflaged ships and teaching at the art school. Harris was instructing in musketry at Camp Borden. MacDonald and Carmichael were in Toronto.

Each must have felt the loss in his own way, none more than Tom's friend, Dr. McCallum. All knew that their plans had received a shock, that only a few of those who read of the tragedy in the newspapers would appreciate what the loss of a comparatively obscure painter meant in the imaginative life of the country.

The body was recovered and taken to Tom's home in Owen Sound for burial, but those who knew him wished to see a permanent memorial in Algonquin Park, the place he cared most about and which his art depicts. Before the summer had passed, MacDonald designed a brass inscription plate and Tom's fellow artists and friends had it set on a simple truncated pyramidical cairn of boulders strongly piled and cemented in a commanding position close to an old camp of the artists on Canoe Lake. The actual physical labour of the greater part of this work was done by J. W. Beatty who was one of Tom's admirers and close associates since the old days at Grip Limited.

The canoeman passing to and from what is known as Joe Lake may see, if he looks, the little cairn shouldering into the skyline above him. The visitor at Mowat Lodge will note it a mile or more across the water, a unique landmark to Canadian genius. One raised with a similar motive stands in the burying ground of Fort Metagami at the northern end of Algonquin Park to commemorate the death of another young artist Neil McKechnie, who knew Thomson and was one of the old staff at Grips.*

Tom's cairn is now on a public waterway of a popular summer outing ground. A boy's camp is not far distant and it may be that the younger generation who go there yearly to learn the craft of the woodsman will see it and ponder the words engraved in brass "To the memory of Tom Thomson, artist-woodsman and guide who was drowned on Canoe Lake, July 8th, 1917; who lived humbly and passionately with the wild. It made him the brother to all untamed things in nature. It drew him apart and revealed itself wonderfully to him. It sent him out from the woods only to show these revelations through his art; and it took him to itself at last."

---

*This paragraph is reproduced from an article by J. E. H. MacDonald in *The Rebel.* November, 1917.

CHAPTER XII

Mentioned in Despatches

JACKSON was wounded at Sanctuary Wood in June 1916. The incident with its associated events has thus been recorded briefly in a Toronto newspaper: "An artist-scrapper is Lieutenant A. Y. Jackson who held down a job as a private in the 60th Battalion in which capacity he stopped a Hun bullet, or a bomb, or a shell (he failed to say which) and hoisted a wound stripe. Later on Lord Beaverbrook grabbed him for the war records, gave him a lieutenant's commission, bought him some paints and told him to get even with the Boche."

What had happened was this.

After being in a hospital in England for months in 1916, Jackson was run through the various casualty depots and was about to return to France. The camp where he was stationed was more like a prison than a training camp. They were dull, humiliating weeks for him. Much water had flowed under the bridges since he and his companion marched through the streets of Montreal under the eyes of the cheering crowds to whom the scene was a spectacle with an extra thrill. Then every man who marched was at his best in physique and morale; the banners, the bands, the flags, the waving hands of friends on the sidelines and a square meal under the belt made war a great and glorious adventure.

Now the battalion was broken up; many were killed; many maimed for life, or gassed, or shell-shocked; others like Jackson were being whipped into shape in camps subsequent to a convalescence.

He had just heard of Thomson's death. His application for a lieutenant's commission had been rejected owing to physical unfitness. The same M.O. passed him as fit to return to France as a private, and he had settled down doggedly to see it through. While digging trenches one day with several others, adding his own quiet curses to the more outspoken ones of his comrades, an order reached him to report to the commanding officer at once.

He was wanted in London. He was to catch the next train. It looked as though there was an art job waiting for him on the staff of the Canadian War Records. Art!—That was a thing he used to work at. Out in Flanders he had hurriedly made an occasional scribble on the backs of letters or envelopes.

Jackson reported in London. Lord Beaverbrook, with the authority of the Logos at creation, said to his secretary, "Make this man a lieutenant"

—and it was so. In 1915, as a private he had kept to the back streets to avoid the humiliation of saluting an officer. Now he took to the byways of London in order to miss being saluted. He was to all intents and purposes out of the army and permitted to enjoy comparative freedom. This was in August, 1917, more than a month after the death of Thomson.

"Are you a portrait painter?" asked Jackson's superior officer.

"No, sir," was the reply.

"Report to-morrow morning at ten o'clock to do a portrait of Corporal Kerr, V.C."

"Yes sir," said Jackson, saluting.

F. H. Varley whom the reader will remember as one of the old Grip tribe was another Canadian artist who received an appointment on Beaverbrook's War Records. Jackson found him striving to depict the likeness of a general who insisted on being painted with his sleeves twisted in such a manner as to display his chevrons.

The idea of the Canadian War Records is understood to have been conceived by the late Sir Edmund Walker and incorporated with the work of Lord Beaverbrook in England. "While one might criticise the general scheme," writes Jackson* "while

*Article in *The Lamps* in 1919.

one might criticise the prominence given to subjects of little importance, the lack of continuity as an historical event, and the divergent tendencies among the artists, it is well to remember that the plan was evolved at a strenuous period of the war, after Vimy and before Passchendaele. The government was not keenly interested, nor the army authorities enthusiastic. Funds had to be found largely through the other activities of the Canadian War Records Office. A definite plan of decoration was not possible in the uncertainty of a half-finished war and rumours that were current of a Canadian army moving to Italy, Russia or Salonika. It was decided to send as many artists to France as the military authorities would allow and thus gather together a lot of vivid impressions of the war; also to commission a series of large paintings of war activities and defray as much of the cost as possible by war exhibitions."

Jackson goes on to point out that the most significant departure from the official attitude toward art, was the granting of several commissions to artists not in sympathy with academic ideals.

"Academic art in Britain," he says "had fallen to such low ebb that even the public had grown weary and the vital or more intense work of the men who expressed ideas found general approval. With a battlefront over four hundred miles long, the literal painter had to choose between a wearisome panorama with minute figures and endless little puffs of smoke, or a mere detail of a battle. The machine gun was found to be an effective weapon for breaking up compositions. The four-square and cavalry mass so effective in older battle pictures was gone forever and the open concentration of a modern battle made necessary another interpretation."

And so, almost for the first time war was painted, not in its barbarous glory but as it is,—hateful bloody, destructive, hideous. There was only one real old time battle-canvas in the collection, says Jackson, "Captain Weirter's 'Courcelette' exciting through its teeming activity rather than through any effective use of line and mass."

The showing made by the Canadian artists in England at this time deserves mention. Though their work was in the minority it did not suffer by comparison with the best British painters. Paul Konody, a London critic, was astonished to find colonial painters so closely in touch with all that is vital in modern art. "When the suggestion was made" writes Jackson "that the Canadian War Records employ Canadian artists, he (Konody) feared the imposition of some timid followers of the Barbizon School, or weak exponents of South Kensington ideals. One expects Colonials to be humble and dependent in the arts, and apart from some of the artists themselves we are decidedly so."

And strange as it may seem, these modern realistic Canadian pictures were popular in Toronto when exhibited there after the war, whereas a few months later when the re-assembled group held an exhibition of Northern Ontario landscape, subjects treated in the same modern fashion, the public were skeptical.

"Up the line one was conscious of so much more than visual impressions" says Jackson. "Hell Blast Corners could look serene and colourful on a spring day, and one could find colour harmonies on the Green Crassier, but these were only minor truths which confused one trying to render an equivalent of something crowding in on all the senses."

A great exhibition of Canadian war memorials was held at Burlington House, London in 1919. The moderns of England and Canada were represented in full war paint. Here were Jackson's and Varley's between Augustus John's and Paul Nash's. The portraits on the whole were not good as works of art for reasons which are apparent from the previously mentioned experience of Jackson and Varley. The painting of the portrait of a pompous general dressed up for the occasion had no particular interest to men who had been depicting the wrecks of battlefields.

MacDonald wrote of the London Exhibition in *The Rebel* taking advantage of the occasion to quote the tributes being paid to the work of his friends especially Jackson's "Hot Mush Stuff", and the paintings of his old Grip associate Varley.

"And another Canadian artist who has had to be discovered for his own people by a British critic is Fred H. Varley" wrote MacDonald with a note of triumph. "Varley has exhibited little in Canada, being too busily employed in making a living by designing for commercial art, to paint much. No example of his art is owned by the Canadian National Gallery, but his work before the war was well known to a small circle who expected great things of him when he and others were sent to England in the spring of 1918 to work for the war records."

Varley, like Lismer, was a Yorkshireman. In the early days of the Canadian movement he was more actively associated with it than at present. As a draftsman perhaps there is not his superior in the group to which he belongs. He visited Algonquin Park with Thomson and early became enthusiastic over the country. He and Lismer were friends of Doctor McCallum and stayed with him at his Georgian Bay home where Varley got material for a fine canvas. It looked as though he would join the others in developing what has come to be called a "school" of landscape painting, but he turned his attention to portrait work in which he has made a name for himself.*

Varley's paintings aroused a lot of discussion in England. In an article in the daily *Telegraph* on the War Memorial Exhibition, Sir Claud Phillips mentions him with special emphasis. "His two works 'When Graveyards Yawn' and 'For What?' show genuine power" said the critic. "There is nothing here of sentiment, nothing indeed of personal passion. We find a massive objectivity, a sense of all-pervading tragedy, of human will overpowered by Fate."

Varley's method is described as "ultra modernism but with little of the fantastic or exaggeration that disfigures the work of post-impressionism." The *Nation* took "For What?" as the text of a sermon entitled "The Picture of the Sphynx" in its issue of January 18th, 1919.

"There is one picture by Captain F. H. Varley of a tip-cart" says the *Nation*. "It is canted on the side of a shell crater which is nearly full of drainage. Beyond it in that winter light, which in Flanders seems to have a quality of indescribable aus-

*Varley, in 1926, became an instructor at the British Columbia Art School in Vancouver.

terity quite alien and outer world, and disciplined with exactitude across a stretch of orcheous muck, is a parade of neat little white crosses. One of a labour battalion leans on his spade and contemplates the cart. More work!—It is loaded with a tangle of legs and arms. The title is "For What?" . . . Who can say? Who dares to put that question not to the world but to himself? It may be that he would rather not examine and rather not know 'for what?' because we are still merely determined to accuse as being the easiest way of solving the riddle."

Then the writer in the *Nation* goes on to say that the question of the soldier artist is rarely as direct as Captain Varley's but that in some ways at this exhibition it always faces the visitor "as in the picture by Lieutenant A. Y. Jackson of a little wood in a salient; the usual stumps of trees with their splinters, the same cold and forbidding light shining on the everlasting mud.—'Copse Evening' the artist calls it in mockery."

These English references to his friends, MacDonald quotes at length. "In such a significant way" he says "are our artists mentioned in despatches. There are others besides the two above, both overseas and at home, but space does not admit their consideration. They will return. They will interpret for us with deeper insight the distinctive beauty of the land they have served. May their countrymen leave the old apathy behind them, the old condescension, the old ridicule slangy or implied, and arouse themselves to an appreciation of their efforts!"

CHAPTER XIII

New Materials

AS the war drew to a close the swells of national feeling ran high in Europe and America. The United States had entered the conflict. Canadian sentiment was stirred with the events of Vimy and Passchendaele. The long lists of casualties published in the daily newspapers added fuel to the national spirit. This feeling affects natures in different ways. With some it arouses the destructive potentialities; with others, the creative. It is as though gusts blow through a multitude of stringed instruments and each responds with music of a different key. Harris, whose brother had been killed in action, was now doing duty at headquarters in Toronto. In him the national spirit of the day provoked a desire to express what he felt about the country in a more creative and magnificent communion than a communion of war. It must be on a grander scale than anything hitherto attempted, heroic enough to stir the national pulse when the stimulus of struggle had been withdrawn. He became nervous and unstrung under the discipline of the machine. His health gave out. In 1917 he received his discharge from the army.

Under orders to rest, the first thing he did was to search out his friend Doctor McCallum. The doctor suggested a trip to Manitoulin Island where he felt they would find the sort of material for which Harris was looking. But the scale of that country was disappointing to Harris and they pushed on to the Algoma district above Lake Superior.

Crossing to Cutter by boat, they caught the train to Sault Ste. Marie and the following morning boarded the Algoma Central Railroad and jumped off at Stop 123 where they spent a few days in a lumber camp and then pushed on to Michipicoten Harbour on Lake Superior.

Algoma is still a wilderness, but as civilization creeps northward and the never-tiring prospector finds new gold fields, and the sportsman each year returns home with stories of its trout streams and big game, gradually this ancient haunt of the bear and the moose which someone has said holds the grandest scenery east of the Canadian Rockies, is becoming partially inhabited.

Through the heart of this country flows the Montreal River, now agitated, now stately, swinging towards Lake Superior through flat and towering landscape as remote in feeling as any part of Northern Ontario.

Further north, if you are following the railroad, is the Agawa Canyon stretching for thirteen miles through a gorge where to see the sky one must throw his head well back. The Algoma country is charted on a grand scale, slashed by ravines and canyons through which run rivers, streams, and springs, broadening into lakes, churning lightly over shoaly places or dropping with roll and mist for hundreds of feet. Granite rocks rise to noble heights—their sides and tops solidly covered with hardwood, spruce and pine, a perfect glory in the autumn. No wonder Harris was delighted.

Thus it came about that in the fall of 1918, the first of a series of box-car parties left the Union Station at Toronto for the wilds of Algoma. In this party were Harris, Dr. McCallum, MacDonald and Frank Johnston, a commercial artist, one of the old Grip group, who for the next three years was closely associated with the movement.

In Sault Ste. Marie a freight car was fitted out with windows, lamps, bunks, stove, water-tank, sink and cupboards. A jigger and canoe were taken along on which to make short sketching trips and another step was made in the adventure of Canadian art. Their conveyance in its palmy days had been an office car for a work gang. On one side of the door, and directly below the window, hung a moose-skull topped with sprays of evergreen and red berries. The present crew painted a design above the head into which were worked the names of each. Beneath it were painted the words *"Ars Longa, Vita Brevis"* having one must admit a most unmodern sound.

They were shunted off on a siding in the northland one hundred and thirty miles north of Sault Ste. Marie. Here, perhaps, for the first time on record the wilderness of Algoma was painted by an artist. The black Agawa flowed quietly below the siding, its banks bordered with deep yellow birch, ash and grey-green alder. The brown bracken grew beside the track and the pine-topped walls of Agawa Canyon rose up into the mist on either side. Those who have not seen it cannot appreciate the unbelievable prodigality of colour. Hear MacDonald describe it.

*"Every day advanced the passing of the leaf and soon our painters had to go in quest of the desirable spot of red. The hills that had been crimson and scarlet with maple were changed to purplish

---

*The description here given was written by J. E. H. MacDonald for *The Lamps,* December, 1919. It describes the second box-car trip to Algoma.

grey. The yellow leaves were following fast. We realized one night of breaking cold cloud that there was a growing moon and we looked at our old star friends from the car door; the dipper lying flat along the spruce tops, and one rare light, bright Capella, dimmed in a jet of aurora. After such a night the trees could resist no longer, and many a one cast off her leaves in a desperate shower. Birch leaves that were a dense yellow in the morning were often grey by night. But the wild cherry leaves still clung as though the high fifes and the violins were to finish the great concert of colour. They were another of the notable little graces of the bush, daintily hung in every shade from palest yellow to deep crimson against the big blue-gold of the Montreal Valley."

There was exhilaration for the sketchers in working by rapid and fall. Every rushing stream was a prompter of song like the running of the tap to the house canary. Two of the rare days of the trip were spent by the workers at the great falls of the Montreal River and they had many a good hour on smaller streams. Winter began to skirmish over the land. Robins and bluebirds worked southward in numbers —and an uncertain string of wild geese occasionally appeared from the north. Daily tramps came across groups of deer apparently choosing winter locations for yarding up. Sometimes the frequent rain turned to light snow and one day from the top of a castle hill 'Amunsten' saw a strong attack by winter the snow sweeping every sign of autumn from the hills in swirling white. When the squall lifted, the near trees stood dripping in melting snow and the hills appeared as though covered with solid mounded ice."†

Like Hell Blast Corners on the salient in Flanders there was much more here to be painted than mere visual impressions, but at this period Harris and the rest of them were more concerned with the amazing opportunities for decorative subjects. The panels Harris brought back from the first two trips are mostly masses of vivid autumn foliage in thick chunks of pigment. There is also a great interest in design suggestive of motives for tapestries and rugs. The North got into his blood. For five successive autumns he went to the Algoma or the Lake Superior country. He found a medium for expression of that for which he most cared in the rolling colour breakers of northern panorama. From now on he strides ahead as though he knew definitely where he was going. Year after year he returns with sixty or seventy sketches, each time more simplified in treatment,

†Jackson was with them on the trip which MacDonald describes here and has painted a canvas of this snow storm in Algoma.

more profound and more philosophic. As we have followed the fortunes of these men we have seen the attacks of the critic descending first on Jackson, then on MacDonald. From 1920 onward it is Harris who baffles the bored mind of the reviewer. As for MacDonald, we shall hear about him at the next O.S.A. show. He painted the wild rivers with a wild technique that had never before been seen in this country.

Here for the present, in the wilderness of Algoma we leave them amid its falling leaves and closing winter. In Flanders the guns cease booming and Jackson prepares to return.

CHAPTER XIV

The Group of Seven

IN the year 1919 MacDonald wrote an article which appeared in the *New Statesman* in England recording the conviction of himself and his friends as to the new direction which the Canadian art movement had taken.

"The Canadian spirit in art" he says "is just entering on the possession of its heritage. It is opening a new world and the Canadian artists respond with a spirit that is very good. This world has not the picture-dealers' tone nor the connoisseurs' atmosphere but it has character attractive to the artist; not often so softly beautiful as ruggedly strong, large, homely, free, and frankly simple in colour."

"The Canadian spirit in art prefers the raw youthful homeliness of Canada to the overblown beauty of the recognized art countries. It aims to fill its landscape with the clear Canadian sunshine and the open air, following faithfully all seasons and aspects and it would make its treatment of them broad and rich attempting to convey the sense of rough dignity and generosity which the nature of the country suggests. Let the reader go if he will (to the exhibition) and feel in the pictures the Canadian spirit in art, striving through sincere expression for a self-determination which will enable our people to make their necessary and fitting contribution to the common art treasures of the world."

The painters convinced a few that a real art movement was under way. "After four years of war and the disappearance of Tom Thomson there is no lack of vigour and variety" said a critic in reviewing the 1919 O.S.A. show. "That is the one vital fact. It means that the local (Toronto) movement in art has come to stay."*

The men themselves believed that in Northern Ontario they had found a country which expressed a dominating note in Canadian environment and the spirit of the country. Why, it has been asked, did they forsake the more pastoral district of old Ontario and go to the wilderness? Our Canadian pasture lands have not yet that racial stamp given by generations of work and peasantry such as the rural landscape of Europe has. Where it has, we find Jackson painting it in Quebec. These men were searching for materials with which to express an experience and they did not find those materials in any land of

*Barker Fairley in the *Canadian Forum.*

gentle sleep-begetting rhythms no matter how beautiful. They demanded something architectural and massive, a form into which they might pour the joy in themselves without breaking bottles with the new wine. Just as European artists have long gone to Europe's past for inspiration, so this Canadian group drew its inspiration from the past of this country, the wilderness.

We now enter what might be called contemporary history. This period marks the date from which the movement has been called a "school." They did not call *themselves* so. The name "school" was given to them by the very critics who upbraided them for taking the name. It became attached to them through the formation of The Group of Seven, so-called because of the seven original member painters. The seven were Lawren Harris, A. Y. Jackson, J. E. H. MacDonald, Arthur Lismer, Frank Johnston, Frank Carmichael and F. H. Varley. Johnston severed his connection with the group in 1922 when he went to Winnipeg to take charge of the art school in that city. Fred Varley, though still a member, has practically ceased to paint landscape for exhibition. MacDonald who found a way out of the routine of commercial art through painting, now, as a teacher of the art of lettering and commercial design at the Ontario College of Art, is giving to commercial art students a new standard for their craft. Carmichael the youngest of them all has, like MacDonald, been compelled to throw intensive effort into the field of commercial art, but he manages each year to complete a few canvases alive with response to northern autumn landscape. In 1926 Carmichael's friend Alfred J. Casson, another young Toronto artist, joined the group and exhibited with them for the first time.

The Group of Seven has never possessed an official head. The story of the events which lead up to its formation as told in the preceding chapters will dispel it is hoped any lingering idea that its founder was Tom Thomson. The Group had no founder. The idea was a joint one, nor had it any ulterior motive to promote it other than a wish to make Canada's spiritual life richer. There was naught to be gained either of fame or money by going to the backwoods and painting in a manner which they knew would be disliked by those who judged their work; nor by launching into an adventure in which they have to this day persisted through ridicule and even slander. They set their conviction against the entire press of the country and the opinion of those whose word was accepted as authoritative in Canada on questions of art. They have encouraged competitors and have consistently refused to be drawn into quarrels.

Their immediate object was to hold exhibitions not only in Toronto but in all possible cities and towns throughout Canada and the United States. As a group the cost of these exhibitions could be evenly distributed among themselves and they could show their work in places where it might otherwise have been impossible.

This outer object has been achieved. Four years after the group was formed their canvases had been exhibited by invitation in practically every important gallery of the United States as far west as Minneapolis. They have toured Canada on more than one occasion and they have been seen in England.

The only oath of allegiance among the members of the group was a determination to be themselves. "We have no group formula and are conscious of widely divergent aims" is stated in the catalogue of one of their early exhibitions. "We have as little desire to be revolutionary as to be old fashioned."

No group formula could reconstruct the mood of Algoma on canvas. It must needs be done by the broadest application of general principles. It must be an adventure in paint. "Art must take the road" —They knew not whither.

It does not seem worth while reviewing point by point the criticism heaped upon the work of these men at the beginning of the group's career. The layman will hardly appreciate their technical problems and time is gradually revealing the puerile nature of earlier objections. These Canadian painters under the stimulus of Northern Ontario landscape recapitulated in a short time the experience of the French Impressionists and post impressionists in Europe fifty or sixty years before them and were as soundly thumped by the press and were given as little credit for any serious purpose other than to startle and win notoriety. They were after a big spirit and a mood rather than a photographic likeness. This mood is "a thing in itself" in Northern Ontario. They had demonstrated for themselves what Taine had said in Paris almost three quarters of a century ago that "art is not representation" and they knew that to represent a subject literally in paint resulted only in a lifeless chromo suggestive of no mood at all. They had long ago rejected the haze and atmosphere of the once popular Dutch and Barbizon schools, simply because Canadian landscape forms show sharp and clear. Then came the decorative period which led to a bolder summarization of detail, a greater stressing of design and more profundity of colour.

When the group came to paint Algoma, the prodigality of nature's materials necessitated still greater summarization and simpler handling. Design became organic in the presentation. Form was organized to meet design. Broken rhythms in nature were connected and modified. The physical part of the picture was made subordinate but contributory to the spirit.

The liberties which the Group of Seven took with nature brought upon them the accusation that they could not draw. The fact that each handled subjects in a similar though quite distinct way on canvas provoked against them the charge that they were following a group formula. Some thought them either crazy or poseurs. The traditionalists spoke of them as "gone astray." The literalists said it did not look like the real nature. Others called them "colour mad" and a freer use of primaries brought the same sort of criticism as Jackson had received in his "hot mush" paintings in 1913.

No one unless he has seen the northern woods in autumn (not merely from a train) can picture to himself the avalanche of colour massed in panoramas or interiors to the most riotous effects. On the side of a hill they spire upwards in explosive puffs or roll in rhythms, forms and patterns that are an untraceable maze of design. Combine this with the wild note of the wilderness: dramatic skies, epic forms reflecting the changing hues borrowed from the woods, and frequently the whole scene mirrored in a lake or stream with a brilliance almost equal to the original.*

Jackson gives us an idea of the problem of sketching in Algoma.†

"Seldom is there found a subject all composed and waiting to be painted. Out of a confusion of motives the vital one had to be determined. Sketching here demanded a quick decision in composition, an ignoring or summarization of much of the detail, a searching out of significant form, and a colour analysis that must never err on the side of timidity. One must know the north country intimately to appreciate the great variety of its forms. The impression of monotony that one receives from a train is soon dissipated when one gets into the bush. To fall into a formula for interpreting it is hardly possible. From sunlight in the hardwoods with bleached violet-white tree trunks against a blaze of red and orange, we wander into the denser spruce and pine woods where the sunlight filters through; gold and silver splashes playing with startling vividness on a birch trunk or a patch of green moss."

"Such a subject would change entirely in ten

---

*The *International Interpreter,* New York, said in 1925: "The strange thing is that these remote unsophisticated painters seem to have caught naturally the child-like vision that the sophisticated poet impressionists sought." (See Chapter XX.)

†The quotation is from the *Canadian Forum* of March, 1921.

minutes, and unless the first impression was firmly adhered to, the sketch would end in confusion. Turning from these to the subtle differences in a frieze of pine, spruce and cedar, or the lighter, graceful forms of birchwoods, one had to change the method of approach in each case. The first demanded fullness and brilliancy of colour; the second depth and warmth; the next subtlety in design and colour; and these extreme differences we would comingle all through."

I am trying to show that in treatment and technique, the Northern Ontario canvases by the Group of Seven were dictated by the country itself. What some mistook for affectation and an effort on the part of the artists to be different was actually an earnest attempt to be sincere and not to permit rules or formulas to make them set down an untruth. By allowing nature to dictate the terms and through the adoption of a receptive creative attitude, the pictures gained a life of their own. By making representation subordinate to other things of more importance they were able to emphasize only form which was significant to mood, composition, design and rhythm. Even texture and finish had its function, for the spirit of Algoma and Lake Superior cannot be depicted with a glass gloss. The group therefore did not in any sense ignore the fundamental laws of painting in making their canvases creative apart from the subject matter before them; nor did they allow themselves to become putterers in a blind alley of professional abstraction into which the layman cannot enter.

I remember one evening after listening to a lecture on the construction of a musical symphony hearing a friend remark, "It has just occurred to me for the first time what the Group of Seven do in their canvases. I have heard Bach's Passacaglia in C Minor described as being in music what a great gothic cathedral is in architecture. Harris's 'Above Lake Superior,' Lismer's 'Islands of Spruce,' MacDonald's 'Solemn Land' and Jackson's 'Moose Country' has this same architectural basis." It is a later achievement assisted perhaps by the monumental type of landscape faced in the north, but fundamentally because the artists themselves apprehended form as "a thing in itself."

Lastly and allied to structure is the emphasis on rhythm. MacDonald can make a canvas rock with it as in his "Wild River" and Lismer sports with it in "September Gale." Jackson makes it the basis of his most intimate sketches. In Harris's work it is restrained but omnipresent. Carmichael apprehends it.

Roger Fry the English art critic in an essay on

the artist's vision refers in an illuminating way to rhythm.* That which he says regarding the creative vision and the manner in which it sees rhythm helps to rationalize the "rhythm" feature of the group's work. Fry writes:

"Almost any turn of the kaleidoscope of nature may set up in the artist this detached and unimpassioned vision. The (esthetically) chaotic and accidental conjunction of forms and colours begins to crystalize into harmony and as this harmony becomes clear to the artist his actual vision becomes distorted by the emphasis of the rhythm which has been set up within him. Certain relation of directions of line become for him full of meaning. He apprehends them no longer casually, nor merely curiously, but passionately; and these lines begin to be so stressed and to stand out so clearly from the rest that he sees them far more distinctly than he did at first. In such a creative vision the objects as such tend to disappear, to lose their separate unities and to take their separate places as so many bits of the whole mosaic of vision."

This creative vision is marked in the landscapes of the Group of Seven. A good example of it is Lismer's canvas "September Gale," the material for which was gathered just off Doctor McCallum's is-

*Vision and Design.

land, Georgian Bay, in one of those dramatic squalls for which the district is famed. Here rhythm, featured in all Lismer's pictures, is carried about as far as he has taken it anywhere. In the foreground is a shaken young pine clinging grimly with its roots to the crevices of some bare rocks. The foam-rimmed waves run through a channel between the pine in the foreground and an island beyond. The sky is a design of moving clouds. It is a fine delineation of movement and rhythm played one against the other and the orchestration of them to a harmonious unit in composition in what a musician might term a contrapuntal fashion. The waves are treated as pure form not unlike the waves of certain Japanese artists and, to re-quote Fry "certain relations of direction of line become for him full of meaning. He apprehends them no longer casually nor merely curiously, but passionately."

This bringing to Canadian art galleries the elemental rhythms of the north must of necessity be of the greatest importance. Perhaps that which most differentiates Canadian landscape, from that of the older art countries is this curious thing, rhythm. It exists here in its elemental form, Nature and the elements being the sole designer. In a pastoral and cultivated country man's tamer and restricted handiwork has marred its sweep. Surrender yourself to the rhythm of the north shore of Lake Superior, the prairies and the Rockies and it will set within you the tempo of the mood Canadian.

To enter a Group of Seven show is to feel power around you. "In these strong and solemn landscapes of the North" says a writer after visiting an exhibition "it was with me as with some watcher of the sky when a new planet swims into his ken. I felt as if the Canadian soul was unveiling to me something secret and high and beautiful which I had never guessed; a strength and self-reliance, depth and mysticism I had not suspected. I saw, as I had never seen before, the part the wilderness is destined to play in moulding the ultimate Canadian."*

I think of the group's Northern Ontario canvases as doing for Canadian painting what the epic poets do for their races. Homer and Hesiod gathered together the unrecorded myths of primitive Greece and thereby a background was lit up for the race which followed. One does not have to throw imagination far into the future to realize that ere long much of what we Canadians now call wilderness will be as myth. A hundred years have seen the Prairies crossed and the north shore of Lake Ontario and Erie become the sites of large cities and

*The Observer in *Toronto Daily Star.*

of a rural population. Already civilization is creeping northward to the James Bay and the country north of Lake Superior gives promise of becoming a great mining area. The wilderness is being reclaimed and the forest is making its last stand. No first class literature has been created to preserve its mood. But in these Northern Ontario canvases is a spirit which as time advances will be capitalized in literature and more recognizable in the race than it is at present. While these pictures live we can never forget our cradle-environment. The work of the pioneer and the explorer and the tenacious love of the red indian for the land of his ancestors will be better understood and the spirit of still unwritten epics will be preserved for us on canvas.

Members of the group have roamed from Halifax to Prince Rupert and have painted the Rockies above the timberline. They go where the primeval spirit of nature still lingers under northern skies and they go where the spirit of new settlements is seen on the outskirts of Canadian cities, or where the roots of Canadian life sink deepest in French Quebec. They have lit a fuse along which the spark will travel to the creative repository of the nation's life. Their movement is to-day about the only activity in Canada providing encouragement to those who desire to see our people liberated from the hypnotic trance of a purely industrial and commercial ideal.

CHAPTER XV

Early Group Shows

THE first exhibition of the Group of Seven was held in the Toronto Art Gallery in the spring of 1920. It was spoken of as "a shock" at the time but several of the canvases have since been purchased for the Ottawa and Toronto permanent collections. The foreword printed on the front of their catalogue has been quoted from freely in this book.

"New materials" it said "demand new methods, and new methods fling a challenge to the old conventions. It is as impossible to depict the pageantry of our northern woods with a lead pencil as it is to bind our young art with conventions and methods of other climates and other ages."

"The thought of to-day cannot be expressed in the language of yesterday. The Victorians seem dull and the Elizabethans frigid to a generation with its own problems. Artistic expression is a spirit, not a method; a pursuit, not a settled goal; an instinct not a body of rules. In the midst of discovery and progress, of vast horizons and a beckoning future, art must take the road and risk all for the glory of a great adventure."

Their first show is described by Bridle as containing in it "tumbling rivers, cataracts, waterfalls and fishing villages; tangled gardens and beaver dams; lone weird rocks and lakes on high levels. . . In colours,—everything—jungles and jangles of iridescence, stacks of blues,—from mauve and violet to ultramarine and deep reds; from super-scarlet and vermillion to the sulky burnt umber that is almost a smudge; yellows, from pale lemon to deep orange; sometimes in the same picture greens from the pale tint of an apple tree bud to the glooms of old-age mosses."

Most of this colour came from Algoma, from the brushes of Harris, MacDonald and Johnston. Varley and Carmichael had not yet painted so far north but the latter had three autumn landscapes which contained most of the colours of Bridle's category. Johnston during his short connection with the group produced a great number of works one of which "Northern Lights" an Algoma picture was shown in 1924 at Wembley. Johnston's particular style of painting was in harmony with the decorative treatment of the others at this period. He was one of the Algoma pilgrims who escaped practically unscathed the pens of the critics. At this first group show he exhibited no less than eighteen canvases all of which one reviewer declares were successful.

MacDonald showed an Algoma canvas he called "The Wild River" by all odds the most striking thing in the exhibition. Bridle in his lurid style describes it as "a canvas of chamelion rocks and scarlet foliage, crooked spruce that suck under stones and a honey-like jazz of wild water half way between a ripple and a foam."

" 'The Tangled Garden' does not seem radical at all" writes another reviewer. "It is gorgeously decorative and looks almost quiet when compared to the explosive canvas 'The Wild River.' In it MacDonald has done a piece of work so far removed from photography and from actual nature (rivers do not flow up hill) that one wonders if Canadian art will ever grow so much more radical that 'The Wild River' will appear as conventional as the 'Tangled Garden.' "*

This picture was painted just below the Montreal River Falls, Algoma, on MacDonald's first trip north. It is a shout of joy. Let the reader rest easy, the river does not flow up hill. It flows with the abandonment of the painter himself when he did it, for this is one of the few times when MacDonald lets himself go and his brush strikes the gait of a genius.

**Mail and Empire.*

"The Wild River" rocks with the vitality and movement of the design. There is the rhythm of the Algoma country. One responds to its daring, its conception, its movement and its significance as a contribution at the time it was painted. It was thought too unrestrained but the Canadian spirit in art had long enough suffered from restraint. It was a broadside of the group announcing as plainly as the foreword to their catalogue that Canadian art had taken the road in search of a definition of that new thing in the world "The Mood Canadian"; the mood which urges one to ask with Whitman "why there are trees I never walk under but large and melodious thoughts descend upon me".

This taking of the road must be understood as an adventure of the spirit. It was, as I say, the beginning of the first serious search for a definition of a mood which members of the group's countrymen feel but cannot define and which will receive its final definition through the medium of human life itself. When it has been sufficiently and clearly defined and felt by all classes it will merge with the universal mood of races.

For three years Algoma dominated the Toronto Gallery and during that period MacDonald under its influence painted, in 1922, his great canvas "Solemn Land." Here the mood is not an emotional revelling in decoration and design but is restrained and austere. "Solemn Land" was painted on the Montreal River, Algoma, under a dramatic northern sky. A steep coast thickly blanketed with spruce and hardwood swings back to a bold promontory of rock in fine light and shadow its granite base rising from the water. The eye proceeds from this central form to hills beyond and is led upwards into a mighty sky.

Lismer, Harris and Jackson also contributed canvases of Algoma. Harris was working on his own. We see him on the eve of a coming-forth. Bridle tells us he had already made two or three attempts to dramatize the north in "a marvelous sunset seen through a screen of red-tinged trees." Each year he returned from Algoma and the work of the previous year looked thin and unsatisfying to him. He was on the point of carrying Canadian painting into a realm where no one as yet has followed.

Algoma was an incident on the road which Canadian art had taken. Its chief importance to the movement was the renewed life which it injected into the men after four years of disorganization. All the members of the group who journeyed northward clarified for themselves the lines along which they afterwards worked. It enriched and deepened their conviction and caused the Canadian critic and Canadian public to think about painting as they had never done before.

With these Algoma years began a procession of exhibitions across the continent in which thousands of Canadians saw for the first time on a large scale a "Canadian statement in art."

CHAPTER XVI

Jackson Paints Again

IN 1918 shortly before the close of the war Jackson was ordered to Siberia with the Canadian army. The order was countermanded a few days later on the sudden signing of the armistice and he therefore returned to Canada to receive his discharge. We find him in Halifax doing work for the Canadian War Records where during intermissions between duties, he roamed out into the precincts of the city and among the villages on the coast of Nova Scotia enjoying the first real sketching on his own account in four years.

On one of these trips he collected the material for "Entrance to Halifax Harbor" the first canvas by a Canadian painter to hang in the Tate Gallery, London, an incident which aided more than any one thing to turn the tide of opposition in Canada toward the work of the Group of Seven.*

On receiving his discharge the ex-artist of the

***Entrance to Halifax Harbor* was bought by the Tate Gallery after being exhibited at Wembley in 1924.

Canadian War Records returned to Toronto having in the meantime been elected a member of the Royal Canadian Academy. "In the year 1919" he writes "the arts in Canada were reduced to the importance of tiddley-winks." He had however temporarily solved his economic problems by savings banked on active service but the too crowded associations of army life seem to have had their re-action on Jackson when at last he was free. During these years he went off by himself, one winter to the Georgian Bay and another to some Quebec hamlet.

Ever since he had visited the Georgian Bay in 1913 the memory of it had remained with him. He had never seen it in winter. Therefore it was that in February 1919, the year he received his discharge from the army, we find him returning to his old sketching ground. It was necessary that, starting from Penetang, he should snowshoe fifteen miles across the ice to his friends the France's in the Freddy Channel where he had met Doctor McCallum six years before. Here he remained until the following April sketching in the coldest weather.

Jackson's name must always be associated with the Georgian Bay. He is always at home in his Georgian Bay and Quebec canvases. The rugged poetry of the two districts is in harmony, though in outer fact they so widely differ. He loves the subtler sensuous beauty of nature and does not depart from the immediate beauty lying before our eyes. This is not to say that he paints a photographic likeness. His summarization and sacrifice of material is always generous. It requires sympathetic discernment to enter into and enjoy the full richness and subtlety of his landscapes. They are dug into and felt over with the utmost tenderness of observation towards the contours and colours of the rocks, the trickery of light and shadow and the rugged rhythm of the entire country represented within the four mouldings of the frame. There is likewise the joy of handling colour and the brush. He is not alone in love with his subject, he is in love with his art. From an academic standpoint Jackson is probably the most accomplished painter of the group. He escapes the handicaps of his technical art training by his honesty and intuition. If he breaks rules he justifies the violation by giving fine structure and design.

"Winter, Georgian Bay" exhibited at Wembley in 1924 is one of the many canvases of this period. I do not single it out as "best" but because here we are given a typical example of a Jackson snowscape. It is a Georgian Bay island in winter loneliness, its growth of crooked pines plunged in drifts. A quick glance will designate the direction of the prevailing wind and as a composer might take that for a motive on which to build a musical structure, Jackson makes it the key to his rhythm. The blanket of snow is spread and smoothed out with a sort of mother-gentleness in accord with the painter's reverence for its whiteness and cool shadows. He loves his nature too much to make her utterly severe even in his Lake Superior canvases. A streak of high light or a blue shadow or the colour of a bit of rock showing through the snow is to him sacred.

The emotional element is always conspicuous. The paint is felt on to the canvas. I know a sketch of his of broken, burnt and rotting stumps of trees which has the power to draw tears. It is like a nature-worshipper's lament over the destruction of his shrines and idols yet so much feeling is firmly, gently restrained and there is never a false note.

He has painted the Georgian Bay in all seasons and in almost every aspect; from its open spaces ruffled by a brisk breeze, to its inmost channels in the delicate lacery of early spring. He finds in the smoothly rounded rocks, colour, rhythm, light and shadow which he never tires of exploring. He camps on off-shore islands, hunts out silhouettes of pines and environs them with night and witchery.

Some one has said that Jackson has done for the Georgian Bay in paint what Sir Walter Scott did in poetry for the Higland Trossacks. Some day perhaps a greater number of people will consent to the comparison. In his more imposing canvases of the north one occasionally feels that he deliberately sets himself a task but in his Georgian Bay and Quebec canvases it is a labour of love. One cannot canoe in and out of the web of channels from Portage Island to Tadenac without passing and recognizing his haunts.

In point of time Jackson's Quebec villages are later than those of the Georgian Bay group but in period they may rightfully be classed together. He himself has told me how he was lured by the seclusion and quiet of French Canada after the wrack of war, and into its delineation he has injected a long deferred peace.

The province of Quebec is Jackson's birthplace. As a youngster at the most impressionable period of his life, Quebec's rhythm was incorporated into his soul. An artist of Jackson's calibre acquaints himself subconsciously with the objective facts of landscape which once felt and understood he may use to suit his purpose as the economist uses statistics. The facts gathered as a boy came useful to the man. Not one of these Quebec pictures show any stress in the doing. An uninterrupted flow and contact between the artist and his subject appears throughout. They are filled with delightful surprises in colour notes; a red roof here, a wooden barnyard cock on a gable and multi-coloured houses. The French Canadian does not stick to conventional methods of painting his home. He chooses the shade that suits him and Jackson may at times have to change it for the purpose of harmonizing his composition.

No one ever described French-Canadian Quebec so well as Adjutor Rivard in his book "Chez Nous" which Jackson has illustrated. Rivard makes the boy ask "What do you think of it Uncle Jean? People keep talking of country; speakers have the words forever on their lips and writers on the tip of the pen. What *is* one's country Uncle Jean?"

"Two or three times he drew at his pipe in silence and blew a cloud of smoke; then with eyes still bent on the distant woods, a wide sweep of his hand embraced the fields, meadows and forests; and thus he spoke. 'Our country—It is that.' "

" 'Over there to the sou' west lives François le Terrien, and beyond him Pierre the son of Denis, and then other neighbours, and other neighbours again. To the nor' east we have the big Guillaume and old Ambrose's two sons; and more neighbours and yet more neighbours to the end of the concession, and the end of the Parish. Now let us say—I do not know precisely whether it is the case but it ought to be, let us say that every man of them like myself is on land that belonged to his people. You would have a whole parish rooted in the soil, wouldn't you? And then in the centre stands the church, alongside it the burying ground; close by the curé's house and the curé himself inside it. After our parish there is another parish, and another, and another, all alike, and each with its church steeple, its curé, its buried dead, its old soil worked by fathers and fathers' fathers which one loves more than oneself. There you have it, this country of ours!' "

This feeling of habitant Quebec which Adjutor Rivard has given us in "Chez Nous" Jackson gives us in paint. He has hundreds of sketches gathered between Levis and Baie St. Paul. He loves to find a winter road where the snow tracks play hide-and-seek around the drifts or where the tops of old snake fences (no telling how old) are just on a level with the snow so that one, if he could balance, might walk along the topmost rail.

And then there is the river, the St. Lawrence, that flows forever out to the gulf with the water of the great lakes and the rivers of northern Ontario. There are the blue hills you see across the river in so many of his pictures. Jackson likes to paint them in the early spring when the snow is patchy on the steeps and the ice is breaking on the river and lumps drift by with the current which the painter can arrange as he likes to suit his composition.

One of his best is "A Winter Road." It is a piece of pure design, yet so much more. You see a collection of tiny gable-roofed houses through a gap in Uncle Jean's snake fence most of which is buried in deep snow. The winter road is two cutter tracks newly broken. The imprint of the feet of Uncle Jean's horse show like buttons down the centre. It does not run straight this road but dips and rises over knolls and winds off to the right by an old windmill and a barn. The picture suggests a lyric poem of exquisite beauty set to appropriate music.

Always he strikes a modest gay note with perhaps a red cutter as a distinctive patch of colour in the foreground from which the eye may travel on through narrow hidden streets and up a big hill at the back of the village where one might easily imagine there lived "un petit bon Dieu."

These pictures make one love the French-Canadian people. They depict old and settled communities of home-loving folk where the strain of life is eased by a simple faith. Their circulation in art exhibitions through the other provinces of Canada should make toward a more brotherly feeling between two great races which it is one of the highest functions of art to bring to pass. They have the sense of being composed with ease and understanding. There is an inevitability of line and a bringing together of forms into relationship which discloses a steady rhythm that runs through them all as unimpeded as the St. Lawrence flows to the sea.

CHAPTER XVII

Lismer

IT will be remembered that Lismer in the summer of 1915 went to Halifax where we left him painting landscapes at Bedford Basin and war pictures of the hulls of camouflaged ships. He also did sketching at Louisbourg and on Cape Breton Island. Shortly after the war he returned to Toronto and became vice-principal of the Ontario College of Art and a member of the Group of Seven. His duties as an instructor hindered him from making extended visits to the north but like the other members of the group it was Northern Ontario landscape that touched him off to a new creative adventure. He had his first contact with the north when he camped out with Thomson in Algonquin Park in about 1913. Early in this book we heard of him visiting J. M. McCallum at the doctor's cottage on the Georgian Bay. He has holidayed and sketched on the north shore at McGregor Bay near Manitoulin Island. He made a trip to Algoma with some of the others in a caboose. He sketched around the town of Mattawa which before the days of Cobalt and the Timiskaming and Northern Ontario Railroad, was the jumping-off place to the mining country of Northern Ontario. He has painted in French Quebec with Jackson on the Isle aux Coudres and Isle D'Orleans, and from innumerable sketches made on these trips, Lismer has built canvases of bold composition and design, rocking with movement and rhythm, and a creative thrill.

"Art" he says, "is a way of life. It is not entertainment, nor professionalism. It is a necessity." There is no domain of life from which he would banish it. Down on the Isle aux Coudres and Isle D'Orleans he found habitant women making hook-mats, homespuns and catalogues, not as articles of service but for the fun of doing them. The women stow their mats and catalogues away in cupboards by hundreds without using them. Lismer claims they are creations of necessity and that the making of them helps these women to live contentedly their remote isolated lives without sinking down beneath the weight of drudgery as so many women do on the prairies who have no creative outlet.

Writing on this subject in *The Canadian Bookman* of October 1925, he says:

"Immigration from Europe brings annually to Canada thousands of persons. In very many instances these immigrants have some form of expression other than the business of agriculture. There must be among them leaders, workers in metal and wood, potters and stone-cutters, fundamental qualities of hand to be turned into labour on the land.

"In our policy of Canadianization, in thinking only in terms of agricultural development, we do not seek to preserve these talents for the upbuilding of a permanent quality in our nation, and yet these forms of expression are of the very heart of permanency. No people of whatever race can establish their lives in a new country unless their needs are considered, especially in the west with the long lonely winters."

This idea of the necessity of the art element Lismer would carry into every avenue of the national life. He has written articles for a business man's magazine urging Canadian manufacturers to originate new designs in textiles, pottery, furniture and other manufactured products. He wants to see the manufacturer, the salesman, the retail merchant and the advertising man get together with the artist and find where the art element in life can play a part. He sounds the spirit of the Group of Seven movement for industry. "Above all" he says "give a chance for the creative idea to grow in Canada and trust to the potentialities of Canadians to think artistically and create usefully." This challenge to the creative is the keynote of his philosophy, and of his pictures.

A Lismer landscape is an involved piece of work indicative of close observation and an alert analytical faculty. His canvases disclose an effort to realize moving fundamental rhythms synthesized from a complex intermingling of lines, colours, forms, lights and planes. His pictures sometimes have the appearance of being carelessly painted but on investigation they are found to be replete with summarized detail and cosmic generalities. Each new work is an adventure, a stepping off, a wrestle with and solving of a problem of synthesis and construction and the more difficult and involved the problem, the better Lismer seems to enjoy it. Intellectually he works with a profound grasp of the laws of aesthetics and of a philosophic theory of art. Intuitively he is directly at home with the mood and overtone of his subject. His ability to place himself 'en rapport' with time and place enables him to enter into the mood Canadian. His canvases of the north like those of his friends in the group are bold in composition and design and conceived in an epic way. He piles rhythm upon rhythm in contrapuntal fashion. His surfaces are not mere surfaces but planes. His colour is not mere bloom, but forms. Colour was not given the same importance in his early work that it is to-day. It is a later development. In his canvas "Happy Isles" painted in 1924, of which no black and white reproduction can give an idea, we get a pure design presentation richly illuminated with glowing colour forms painted with the ardour of Van Gogh. His landscapes move us by their power, enthusiasm, boldness of conception and execution; by their rhythm and dramatic handling; by their trueness to mood, their architectural plan and their infectious spirit; by their "huskyness" some one has said. Although they are far removed from the literal and photographic, they are accurate as to spiritual fact and sing with the creative adventure of a painter painting and a poet responding to nature.

I am not sure whether it was Algoma or a stormy Georgian Bay that inspired his first effort to tackle epic subjects. Both districts challenge a painter to conceive grandly and cast his spirit to the winds. While visiting Doctor McCallum on the Georgian Bay he did a sketch for a large canvas shown at Wembley and now owned by the Canadian National Gallery entitled "September Gale" to which reference has already been made.* This picture was one of the five selected from the Wembley Exhibition by the Tate Gallery Committee in 1924 to be considered for purchase. When it was bought by the Na-

*See Chapter on Group of Seven.

tional Gallery at Ottawa it raised a storm of protest for its unconventional handling. No painter has given us a truer summary of the spirit of the Georgian Bay in a storm than Lismer has in this canvas. Opposing rhythms are played one against the other in crashing but harmonious relationship. The running waves are felt as modelled forms somewhat after the manner of Japanese painters. Line, plane and form are all significant and alive.

The subject specially lends itself to epic treatment. The field is big and elemental; the detail permits bold synthesis and simplification by summary, and the spirit of the Georgian Bay in storm has a cosmic mood. Lismer looks for and feels these things. "The Georgian Bay" he writes "is stripped of ornamental trappings of the traditional and representative forms of expression, land, water and sky and all the limitless phases of movement and change in and on these elemental areas. The artist must be fundamentally aware of the potentiality of these basic things; be the playground as it were of natural effect. The so-called natural effects are not of the kind that would operate amongst verdant woodlands, or merely pastoral uplands. One is bound to see bigger and more epic forms revealed under the attack of powerful phases of wind and weather, sunlight or season on such a background. To the adventurous therefore the bigger the field the more elemental the effect; the greater the power to sense cosmic design and not representation to record it."

The creative artist in handling the material of effects becomes a cause. Lismer's "September Gale" is a Canadian nature mood made grander in its passage through the medium of the painter's feeling. He has inhaled the gale and exhaled it as his own breath, thereby making a localized subject a timeless symbol of storm.

"Islands of Spruce" sketched on Sand Lake, Algoma, in 1921 is a creation in a quieter mood but here again the painter's idealism raises a typical northern scene to the level of heroic allegory. The dark form of the island rises like the gables of a gothic temple from a base of rocks and perfectly still water which reflects the forms. In the background, on the hills stands a choir of trees each one a rhythmic repetition of the central motive. Bridle called them "a few swats of symbolism masquerading as spruces." The canvas has an architectural quality suggesting pictorially the development of a symphony.

There are places in the north where the startling sense of unseen presences abound. There is a lake in a remote corner of Algonquin Park where prosaic campers who would vigorously resent the suggestion of a belief in denizens of the unseen have admitted unwillingness to spend the night. An invisible forest life, not the animals, seethes in the virgin bush pressing in upon the imagination and making the stranger uneasy. One feels it a little in Lismer's "Islands of Spruce" so still, so dark, so lonely and remote.

"Happy Isles" was done in a corner of the Georgian Bay which none of the other group members have painted, a deep inlet on the north shore in the region of Manitoulin Island known as McGregor Bay. Here the character of the country differs from that farther south. You are close to a range of high hills, the Cloche Mountains. The Bay itself is overshadowed on the north by a white quartz range seven or eight hundred feet in height. Channels writhe in and out among the rocky islands and quickly turn to careering whitecaps when ruffled by the wind. The islands which clutter the bay rise high and sheer from the water. They are really partially submerged foothills.

"Happy Isles" is a great canvas; one of the boldest and most intense in execution that the Group of Seven has so far produced. The painter abandons himself to an emotional orgy of colour. Detail is radically summarized and no stroke remains that has not a definite purpose to perform in the composition.

Every ornament of landscape is stripped away save for a few sparsely clad trees silhouetted at strategic points as a balance or a peg on which to swing a rhythm. Forms are modelled with a line and repeated as a motive with the rapidity of running waves.

The scene is McGregor Bay, a rocky shore and untidy shoals of islands backing away to high dark madder hills on fire with a conflagration of soaring clouds whose orange and yellow glow illuminates the landscape beneath in modified tones of itself, and silhouettes trees as almost black. Behind the blaze of clouds in the upper background are wide patches of deep and silver blues, the darks repeated in the water. It is impossible adequately to describe it or to reproduce its effect and its mood in a black and white print.

"Happy Isles" is a canvas one can respond to as he would to music. Lismer has pointed out that no one asks music to be representative of sounds associated with nature and everyday life. Why then should we demand that a picture be a photographic likeness of a place or a locality? Cannot a symphony of harmonized colour be enjoyed as readily as a symphony of sound? One who has profoundly felt northern landscape can visualize (if one may use the word here) what it might be in music.

LISMER

"Canadian artists" says Lismer "are not dealing with the merely transient, but aiming to give a sense of the eternal." The Eternal is impersonal and timeless and Lismer's best canvases, while their place and time are specifically Canadian, burst through to the timelessness which is the feature of all great art. In his painting of an old tree on Split Rock off Doctor McCallum's island one feels that he has studied the anatomies of all trees, and felt their joints and experienced the throes of their creation. It is an allegorical tree. In it he has gathered up the epic spirit of innumerable great trees which have been wounded by storms and healed themselves again, yet it is a Georgian Bay tree as he who knows the breed will recognize. "September Gale" is not only a local gale on the Georgian Bay. It is "a storm" disassociated from locality. "Happy Isles" is McGregor Bay but also an abstract "happy isles".

Again we see the seeming anomaly that all art which is racial and truly national in spirit becomes universal and timeless, that is, eternal. Keats once said that every man's life is allegorical. The same is true of the life of a nation, the spirit of which being expressed through the work of its landscape painters, hovers over the painter's creation like the living spirit of the human body.

CHAPTER XVIII

Harris's "Above Lake Superior"

IN the populous centres of Ontario the anchorage of a tradition is absent. It is Harris who feels the life of these cities, reads biographies on front doors and is a vagabond of the streets with his brush and his palette. From the first as we have seen, he painted shacks and city streets. He returns to it zestfully again and again partly I fancy to refresh his contact with humanity from which an artist, as wedded as he to the abstract and the subjective, may easily cut himself adrift. He knows that in isolation the artist ceases to be the focus for the spiritual life of his people.

The same critics who recoiled from an art having the backwoods for its inspiration, similarly recoiled when Harris years ago utilized for art purposes the materials of the back streets. But one does not have to know anything about esthetics to feel with Harris for humanity. Sometimes he paints a working man's community on the borders of the city putting into it the spirit of adventure and the creative outlook on life which are the bases of his art and philosophy. The Quebec peasant is the product of a background but these workmen whose homes Harris paints are the makers of one.

Each picture has something in it of the struggle for existence and with this struggle is shown the manner in which the dwellers within the houses face it. Frequently it is the cheerful carelessness of people who really live the doctrine of taking no thought for the morrow. At other times we see how the grind of life is telling and a group of poorly-clad shacks huddle together in winter like sheep in a storm. The brave and cheery lights twinkling through the windows do not deceive us.

These houses by Harris give us an insight into many lives. The genius of the pictures is, that one house as he paints it, helps us to understand intimately the social class to which its inhabitants belong. There is a certain sort of home aptly illustrative of this, a blocky red brick species in the so-called more respectable part of the city. It has a solidity, an absence of swank and a suggestion of conservative but come-as-you-go hospitality which is a distinctive trait of this order of Canadian. Red bricks and white snow and a happy pattern of trees or falling flakes give us that bright-coloured cheer which through the Group of Seven's pictures is becoming more and more associated with things Canadian.

The same end is achieved in three or four canvases of rural Ontario homesteads. Here Harris picks a type of dwelling expressive of the cooky-making, pie-baking farm atmosphere which many Canadians associate with their grandmothers. And the painter does not omit a certain note of puritanical respectability felt at country church socials, a world, the confines of which are the township's concession roads. All this is suggested by treating a characteristic old Ontario farmhouse in a decorative way. There is the wide verandah where the owners sit and watch the neighbours drive along the road. There is the big lawn which Pa may have to scythe a couple of times each summer or perhaps cut with the hay mower. And there is that most characteristic old Ontario touch, the white curley-cues at the top of the verandah posts with which the old English ship carpenters who cleared the land and settled the province decorated their homes.

The use of decorative design was never put to better use than in his ward and slum pictures. The Jews who live in the ward are not a melancholy people. They have a hilarious gayety of temperament which offsets their race's temperamental melancholy. They enjoy community life. Rarely do we find the Jew a farmer. They crowd by preference into closely confined districts of cities unless they are rich enough to ape the opulent gentile.

So Harris paints the ward in bizarre colours and posterish design introducing pink fences, purple doorways, green window sashes, blue shutters and red clothes hanging from the sills. On top of this he floods sunlight and shadow bringing out subtleties of colour in the patchy roughcast walls. He welcomes in his heart both jew and gentile and accepts them as they are with a friendly gesture which speaks the essence of a democratic faith.

His two canvases "Elevator Court" and "Black Court, Halifax" are of a different order from those already mentioned. These Halifax pictures were painted at a period in Harris's life when so distinct a change is marked in his work that everything since done may be easily divided from that which went before. This change shows itself outwardly by an abandonment of the decorative two-dimensional design for that of solid three-dimensional form and restrained colour. Less obviously, it is apparent by the plus quality of a philosophic idealism and more emotionally considered surfaces.

In these two canvases a bitter note appears. They angered a banker, because the spirit of them cries for change, and holds in disrespect and contempt the glory of acquisitiveness which makes an "Elevator Court" or "Black Court" possible.

In each is shown a bare alleyway court surrounded with shells of dingy wooden buildings where people live. The cracks of the clap-board are black rays and overhead thick clouds deepen the depression. In one, small children who have forgotten how to play, make bitterer the artist's comment. In another a cold breaking light intensifies the mood.

The Halifax canvases are shattering to any form of shallow idealism. A naked material fact stares us in the face presented with so much humanity that one reads clearly the experience of the painter in his work. So intense a portrayal of subject could not have been achieved without leaving scars upon the emotional nature of the artist. For the realization must have forced itself upon Harris that Elevator and Black Courts typify the daily life of more than one half of the human race. It must also have been made plain to him that it likewise symbolized a consciousness of spiritual poverty in a very large portion of the remaining half of mankind since were man conscious that he possessed the spiritual resources with which to meet and right Black Court conditions he would do so.

As a contrast, from Halifax in the summer of 1922, Harris went in the fall to the north shore of

Lake Superior where the solitude is creative and the spaciousness elicits the soul's expansion. In Algoma where he had his first contact with the country above Lake Superior, he gives us, as in his shacks, a decorative objective rendering of autumn mostly, though by no means always, in two dimensions. At times he trusts himself farther. As the spirit of Algoma drew him, he comes out from the riotous wood-interiors into the more open country and begins to feel in and around the landscape. The hilarious colour-motives of the woods are surrendered for expanse and form. On the north shore of Lake Superior this is developed. A solemn and austere note enters. Light as a spiritual quality is introduced. There is a settling in, a restraint, a different application of paint, an evener rhythm, and a more careful moulding of forms. The mood is peaceful and back of this peace is a conviction about life, for the mood is sustained through canvas after canvas. We get panoramas, rocky, weathered coastlines and skies of white-grey coldness and silver or golden light. Artists in all ages have painted nature from a spirit of devotion toward her but Harris paints the Lake Superior landscape out of a devotion to the life of the soul and makes it feel like the country of the soul. All of his landscapes are lofty and large in conception. Forms are moulded and felt without a suggestion of sensuality.

The architectural rhythms have the slow, steady flow and aloofness of a wide river.

As in his shack pictures Harris can acquaint us with a whole strata of society through the presentation of a single type house, so in his Lake Superior canvases we can learn the rhythm of entire tracts and regions from one landscape. He guides the eye through the design majestically on the swing of long and positive lines. Very often in the foreground of his pictures rocks are piled up in sunlight their complex systems of crevices and planes summarized in a few rhythmic shadows that impart a sculptural quality. Nearby, almost surely, there will be a naked tree the type of millions of its northern neighbours. In that tree is the background of the wilderness, the history of mighty storms, bush-fires, and the coming of the axemen. He loves to spill light on water or over hills to make austerity serene. In his summary of forms he adheres to the architectural facts of his country. The element of structure is present in a conspicuous degree and a satisfying sense of unity and relationship of design within design and form within form is prominent throughout his best compositions.

In his canvas "Above Lake Superior" he has gathered to himself the oversoul of that wilderness which rolls from Superior's coast to the Hudson

Bay. Five of those trees to which I have just referred, stripped by fire and ice, their white trunks glorified in the glow of northern light, form the forepart of the canvas. Another tree lies on the ground as it were with its face downwards in the spot where it fell, while a forked stick raises a crooked body to receive the descending rays. The pyramidal crown of a purple hill swells up behind the trees beneath ribs of cold gray clouds. Back of this peak, unseen, lies the wilderness. The mood is static, lonely, eternal and austere.

People either love it or hate it. When Leon Bakst the Russian artist saw it he exclaimed "It is not painting, it is sculpture". An Oxford Ph.D. described it as "a horror". A little Irish woman spoke of it as "The Place Where the Gods Live". One man said that Harris should have been locked up for painting it. Another referred to it as a picture of "The Top of the World". It summarizes locality, yet is no locality. It is the North's being. A flowing emotional quality is absent but the emotion of this picture is in the power of its intensity which is directed and subjected to a mood of emotion sublimated beyond fluxiousness and agitation.

Considered as a piece of landscape painting only the work is in summary what its name declares,—the country above Lake Superior. The man who painted it must have absorbed into himself the effulgence of the aurora borealis. As a piece of technical virtuosity Leon Bakst without intending a compliment, paid it his tribute when he said "It is not painting. It is sculpture." One might says also "it is architecture" but the fact remains *it is painting* and as such, analyzed as to its composition, design, colour-harmony, tone-values, form and the relationship of these composite parts to each other, it cannot be dismissed as lacking. As to its power of execution, its enemies must cede that. As to its mood of severity, loneliness and ecstatic peace, some may not like that. But it is after all a mood which Harris chose to hold up before the eyes of men and he has made use of a painter's knowledge and technique to express what he desired and there is not a false note in it. His friend Lismer has pointed out that in standing before a work of art, it frequently judges us more than we it. "Above Lake Superior" is such a work. From one standpoint it is a challenge; a call to the creative in man. It embodies a philosophy of the north. It judges us as individuals and as a people. If we feel its bleakness and hate it, it is our own inner bleakness that hates, the finite part of us that dares not meet that infinite unfathomable thing,—the wilderness.

"Above Lake Superior" must be judged by other than historical standards of art. There is that in it which lifts it out of the moulds of art *qua* art into the realm of a rare experience, a mystical experience which few who have seen the canvas will have shared. This I think explains the baffled confusion and extraordinary dislike which art-lovers of no little discernment have felt before it, and also the fact that the informed art critic sees there the ignorement of the laws he knows though he will find a profound employment of the principles which govern pictorial design.

Harris is a modern mystic who has attempted to express through painting, moods reached through mystical experience as William Blake did. The nature of this experience must have been the product of his humanitarianism which caused him to go out and to feel in a new way with and for humanity as is shown in his Halifax canvases. It is from this base that mystical experience occurs and in a flash of that misunderstood word "illumination", peace comes through a vision which makes it plain that "every moment of life is filled with eternity" and that the uglinesses of Time are ways to a realization of untemporal beauty. The uglinesses of "Above Lake Superior" are beautiful and its lonely austerity, peace.

I believe that we shall see more of this kind of expression attempted in the art of the future, especially here in America. There is no experience common or uncommon, to the few or to the many, which may rightfully be exiled from expression in art. If the historical concept of art be not spacious enough to include in its circumference the whole adventure of life then let us expand our conceptions and definitions and generously admit the universe itself.

CHAPTER XIX

Covering Ground

IN the summer of 1924 Harris and Jackson went sketching in the Rocky Mountains. They covered the section around Jasper Park looking for material as prospectors search for gold, not sticking to the well marked trails, but climbing above the timber line into snow. The travelling was done with camp kit, sketch box and panels. After the timber was left, this load was added to by the fact that they had to carry fire wood. Trips were made to Maligne Lake, to the Athabaska Valley, where they climbed to 8,000 feet, and to the Tonquin Valley, which took them on a journey of nearly twenty miles through the MacCarib Pass.

"We had our first trip," writes Jackson. "It was good fun, though I was short of wind and sore in the heels. We went to Maligne Lake with Lawren,* the guide, four horses and me. I am not used to riding and walked most of the way, about twenty-five miles. We arrived at the fire-ranger's cabin and spent a couple of days with him, then, in a big eighteen-foot canoe, we paddled down Maligne

*i.e., Harris.

Lake fifteen miles and landed on a gravel beach where we pitched the tent. Later we looked down on our camp from two thousand feet up and several miles away. Lots of driftwood for a fire and water right off the near glaciers; flowers all about us, many we had never seen before. On both sides of us, a few hundred yards away, milky glaciers came hurrying over great gravel deltas into the lake."

"In the lake, not a fish, not even a minnow, not a weed growing in the water. When you waded in up to your knees you lost sight of your feet. And towering above us on all sides were great crumbling mountains like the ruins of a gigantic Ninevah. One big pile of remains just opposite the tent looked like six mouldy old sphynxes sitting in a row; Aztec warriors; Pueblo dwellings".†

Another day they climbed up beyond the timber line and kept on into the snow of what Jackson calls the Eastern Ridge. "We stopped for lunch," he says, "about five hundred feet from the top. The rain started, and to get the fire going we had to lean over it and keep it from getting drowned. We got soaked and smoked at once. With the last little stick the water in our kettle started to bubble and then we resolved to at least see the promised land in the rain and climbed on up."

†From a letter to a friend.

The rain stopped. The sun came out, and from the top of the ridge in the sunshine they looked down over a cubist's paradise of red, orange and grey rock and sharp cliffs running in long diagonals, and glaciers sprawling down the treeless valleys;—"a land," says Jackson, "as remote as the far side of the moon".

They got out their sketch boxes and began to work. A cloud swept down upon them. It broke, pouring out rain, hail, sleet and wind and left them with the water running out of their boots. Later a second trip was made to this same country, where camp duds were packed five thousand feet up and a sojourn was made of ten days.

While Harris and Jackson were crawling like ants along the snowy ridges on the edges of glaciers, another member of the Group of Seven, MacDonald, was working in the valleys under the steeps of Mount LeFroy and the waterfalls of Oesa, around Lake O'Hara. In the same region is Mount Victoria, Mount Huber, Wiwaxy, Cathedral, Ringrose, Hungabee and Oderey. And MacDonald wrote, "For nineteen days I wandered in the neighborhood of Lake O'Hara. I looked at the emerald and violet of her colour. It is emerald and malachite and jade and rainbow green, and mermaid's eyes, and the beads of Saint Bridget, and the jewels of St. Patrick's crown and anything else the imagination can ascribe to it. I have waterfalls and glaciers and mountain brooks, and meadows, and rock-slides, and snowy peaks; and there are trees, the spruce and the balsam and the plumy lyell's larch—and August went out in Christmas card weather with the larches all drooping in a sparkle of snowy boughs and sunlight. . . And there were grey cold days when one heard echoes of chaos and cold night on the upper slopes and the spirit of desolation wafted coldly about the rock-slides, and one found the sight of even a little old dried horse dung a consolation and assurance. On such days, and often in the calm still weather, one felt that the mountains are not completed. The builders are still at work. Stones came rolling and jumping from the upper scaffolding and often from the chasms one hears the thunderings as the gods of the mountains change their plans. In these great places all the functions of Nature are on a big scale and the material workings of the frost and wind and rain and sun are clearer to us".‡

Varley, another member of the group, was in the mountains in this year, but he made no sketches. The physical problem of accessibility which the Rockies present to the landscape painter are no less imposing than the problem of getting them on can-

‡*Canadian Bookman.*

vas. "A mighty mountain painted with a photographic likeness may be a very trifling affair," Jackson wrote in the *Canadian Forum* on his return. "The mere representation of nature is nowhere so ineffective as in the paintings of mountains. Cezanne's dictum that 'art runs parallel with Nature and has laws of its own' would seem to have a peculiar application in such a country."

Harris got a fine canvas from Maligne Lake which he exhibited at Wembley in 1925, a bold design sweepingly simplified. In another exhibited the following year in Toronto, he breaks away from anything representational and carries out an abstract conception of mountain forms disassociated from locality. This canvas is almost a combination of sculpture, painting and pictorialized music. It pushes Canadian art another mile along the road which it is travelling.*

But the mountains have not weaned Harris and Jackson away from Northern Ontario. The autumn still sees them camped on the north shore of Lake Superior. For Harris, the region is inexhaustible and he has returned there every season since his first trip to Rossport in 1920. For four years he and Jackson went alone. In 1925 Carmichael joined them. One

*This canvas is called "Mountain Forms" shown at the Group of Seven exhibition in Toronto, in 1926.

year Harris and Jackson camped at Port Munro, about five miles from Port Coldwell.* They rented a rowboat at Coldwell to lift their stuff over to the camp and remained for a month with two weeks of zero nights. They had to knock the snow off the silk tent to prevent the material from tearing and Harris had to break the ice on Lake Superior to get the boat back to its owner when it was time to come home.

One of their methods of getting food was to fish. Jackson caught trout with a heavy piece of cord and an iron railroad spike for a sinker. Another article of diet was blueberries. The chief industries of Coldwell and Port Munroe are fishing and picking blueberries. In a good year, the Indians in the neighbourhood ship out a couple of thousand baskets of berries. In the late fall of 1925, when Carmichael was with them, their camp was at Jackfish and Coldwell. They made a trip to Slate Islands in a gasoline launch with a fair sea rolling over a seven mile strip of Lake Superior. Here they camped and sketched a few days and then returned to Port Coldwell and explored the heights in the neighbourhood as far as they could travel from day to day, from sun-up to sun-down. On one occasion they lost their way and were driven by a blizzard from sketching on the heights.

---

*They were again at Port Coldwell in the fall of 1926.

COVERING · GROUND

An interesting development of Carmichael's first trip to Lake Superior was his breaking into water colour. He had been experimenting in it for years, each time returning to oils with the renewed conviction that water colour was too thin a medium with which to express the powerful moods of Northern Ontario landscape.

Circumstances have kept Carmichael in an office when the others were faring to the wilds. His brief holiday recesses have been spent on motor-camping trips. With camp equipment and sketching material he drives northward in the fall when the colour is bright and in this way has covered accessible parts of the Ottawa valley around the town of Mattawa at the forks of the Ottawa and Mattawa Rivers, about twelve miles north of the northern boundary of Thomson's old sketching ground, Algonquin Park.

For years Carmichael, who has a fine sense of design, moved excitedly in colour and pattern feeling it in a decorative, rather two-dimensional way, but as he pushes farther into Northern latitudes, he begins to feel form more emphatically. The introduction of it into his canvases brought a modelled depth and power, the feeling changing from a lyric to a more epic quality.

His visit to Lake Superior in 1925 was his first

taste of real remote north country. The north shore of Superior, around Jackfish and Port Coldwell, is as austere and remote as anything east of the Rocky Mountains. The skies, the great pitching lake, the bold, stern coast country with its big design motives, drew a response from Carmichael that no other landscape ever had. He thought he could get his feeling about it into water colour and was successful. The work he brought home was the Lake Superior country and no other.* The form element stood prominently forth and simplification and definiteness of outline added power to the design. The magic of the north had touched him off to a new creative adventure. It got him as it gets all who come to know and feel it and at the Group of Seven exhibition in 1926, he showed some Lake Superior canvases in oils which are a new world for Carmichael.

Thus Canadian art keeps on the road. Outwardly it appears to move slowly on its course as the planets and stars seem to move. Perhaps, like them, it travels faster than one thinks. There is no end to the road, no blazed trail; it weaves and winds behind and under the agitated life of the national consciousness and from its trodden places there rises an effulgence illuminating the background of the Canadian people.

*A canvas from this trip, "Northern Village," is reproduced at page 26.

COVERING · GROUND

As the movement spreads the painters gather new materials from out-of-the-way nooks and corners, east and west. In 1923 MacDonald spent six weeks sketching at Petit Riviere, a fishing village on the Nova Scotia coast. Jackson, the roamer, strikes his roots deeper and deeper in the soil of old Quebec. Letters written back to friends give sketchy word-pictures of the haunts he visits. In 1923 he writes from Baie St. Paul,—"There is a good deal of the primitive here yet, thatched barns and many timber houses and a few old stone ones. It is a very beautiful place, almost too much so for painting. The ready-made composition has to be avoided. The railroad came only four years ago, but it is opening the place up to civilizing influences which will not improve it inwardly or outwardly. Already there are four or five houses in stock catalogue architecture and they are likely to set the style and the Ford car will supersede the old cariole. The women still make rag and hook rugs and a little homespun. The rugs are rather interesting. The instinct for colour is quite decided."

And again the same year he writes from Les Eboulements. "I came down here for a week from Baie St. Paul. It is about six miles down the river on the gulf, at this spot eighteen miles wide. A couple of hundred years ago one of the hills slid out into the river, making a cape or point about six hundred yards or so beyond the general shore-line. It is all undulating little frills or 'eboules' I suppose. There is some local joke about its being caused by the Tremblays,—most of the people here bear that name and 'tremblement de terre' means earth-quake, which I don't need to explain. The village is in two parts and likely to remain so for some time, as the upper part is three miles from the lower, and a thousand feet above it. I went to Eboulements en Haut yesterday. It was almost lost in mist. The old church poked its spire into the clouds. We had an exciting run back to the lower town. I put my snowshoes under my arm and got on the back of Gagnon's skis and we fairly flew."

Another time he gives a peep into a French habitant home. "I have a nice chromo above my bed," he wrote from one place, "with an eye in the centre and below it 'God Sees All', and around it are little illustrations of good and evil. An immaculate young man giving a cent to a blind beggar stands for virtue, and on the other side a young gentleman pounding the head of another young gentleman with a large club stands for evil. And below, little angels around the death-bed of virtue and little devils around the bed of the less considerate youth."

Jackson has become an authority on Quebec and on the life of the French habitant as well as on the

Ontario north country. In 1925 Lismer joined him with C. M. Barbeau who was out collecting old French folk songs for the Dominion Government's archives. On this trip sketching was done at St. Hilarian, Baie St. Paul, Les Eboulements, Murray Bay, Isle aux Coudres, Isle D'Orleans and Ste. Anne de Beaupre.

CHAPTER XX

Spread of the Movement

THERE are many signs to-day of the outward advance of the Group of Seven movement in the way of invitations to exhibit, newspaper articles, and the changing attitude of certain sections of the press due primarily to the success scored at the 1924 British Empire Exhibition at Wembley, England.

Since 1921 there have been few months in each year when somewhere in Canada or the United States exhibitions of the Group of Seven were not being held. These exhibits were received, sometimes with enthusiasm, sometimes with ridicule. Since the exhibition held at Wembley, however, when Jackson's canvas "Entrance to Halifax Harbour" was purchased by the Tate Gallery, London, and the press of England united in a chorus of praise over the work of the Seven, signs of a genuine and widespread interest at home are commencing to appear.

Curiously enough, the first place where the pictures made an appeal in Canada was not in Toronto nor any of the larger centres of population, but in some of the smaller cities of Ontario.

SPREAD · OF · THE · MOVEMENT

Shortly after the war, the city of Sarnia decided to start a permanent collection of Canadian pictures. This decision was the result of the efforts of the Womens' Conservative Art Commission, a body of workers, who during the war, had banded together to raise funds for war charities. After the armistice, it was decided to turn the activities of this organization into other channels. Sarnia now has pictures in its permanent collection, all of which are of the modern Canadian school, though not all confined to the members of this Group. Other cities are now becoming interested and a system of circulating art exhibits is being established including London, Chatham, Sarnia and Owen Sound, the birthplace of Tom Thomson. Several of the Group's pictures are distributed in Fort William and Port Arthur. It would be surprising if this were not so, since these cities are in the Lake Superior country.

The movement has also won supporters on the prairies and in Vancouver, where its old friend Mortimer Lamb was asked in 1925, to deliver a course of lectures on Canadian art at the University. In 1923 an exhibition of the Group's work was held in Calgary and *The Trail,* a publication of the Alumni Association of Alberta University, reviewed it in a manner which showed that the younger generation at least felt that here was the Canadian spirit. "We are the heirs of a long tradition in European art," said *The Trail,* "but it has not *our* beauty. . . That intangible sum-total of our own ways of living, our own environment and our own response to our own problems cannot be the spirit of other lands and other times. . . Canadians have wanted a national art. It has come, but Canadians are disappointed because it is not still-born. Canadian art is alive. . ."

At various points throughout the country small public art collections are being established all of which, if not directly connected with the Group of Seven's activities, are nevertheless part of the movement toward which they provided enthusiasm and stimulus. In the city of Brockville, Ontario, in 1924, a friend of the movement organized a group exhibition not to promote the sale of pictures, but to try and interest the schools. Arrangements were made for children under sixteen years of age to vote on each picture and the sketch obtaining the greatest number of votes was presented to the library by its painter as the beginning of a collection. It was one of Harris's that stayed.

In the United States during 1921 and 1922 exhibits were sent by invitation to public galleries in Rochester, Columbus (Ohio), Detroit, Cleveland, Toledo, Minneapolis, Worcester, Massachusetts and Boston. In 1923 and 1924 another show of thirty-six pictures of the Group of Seven travelled the largest cities in the eastern and mid-western United States, ending up in the Brooklyn Gallery. Again it was the younger generation who were impressed. A former teacher of the art school in Detroit told me that he received letters from his students in a number of the different states wishing to know more about the Canadian movement.†

Neither England nor any of the countries of Europe have yet seen an exclusive group exhibition. The success won at Wembley in 1924 and 1925 was only on a few canvases intermingled with those of other Canadian artists not belonging to the Seven.

Wembley was a day of rejoicing among the group's friends, not so much because of its being an answer to carping criticism at home, but because it was the first time that these Canadian artists had had an opportunity of exhibiting, side by side with other painters in other parts of the empire, and because their work was seen and judged by critics familiar, in a way which ours are not, with the best modern work of Europe. Of the many reviews written on the Palace of Fine Arts at Wembley, there was scarcely a writer who did not single out the canvases

†As this volume is on the press a number of the Group of Seven's canvases have been shown at the Sesqui-Centenial exhibition in Philadelphia and have provoked favourable comment. They were also shown at Los Angeles, Cal., in 1925 along with other Canadian artists' work.—(Author).

of these men and declare with conviction that in Canada alone the art of the Empire had "taken a new turn."

The Morning *Post,* which fourteen years before had described a Canadian show as lacking any original form of expression "because of the necessity of seeking the means of expression in the ateliers of a foreign land far from the inspiration of native history, types and environment," on this second occasion of commenting on a Canadian exhibition declared that "there is emerging a native school of landscape awaiting a wider recognition abroad"—and as "having the foundation of what may become one of the greatest schools of landscape painting".

This paper which in 1910 had pointed out that "the observation of the physical fact is strong but the more immutable essences of each scene is crushed out by a foreign begotten technique," in 1925 wrote "In their pictures are new signs of vision and feeling for the spiritual significance of nature in both its static and dynamic moods".

Another London paper, the Daily *Chronicle* said, "These Canadian landscapes are the most vital group of paintings produced since the war—indeed in this century."

The *Field* wrote, "Canada has arrived. She has a national style, however young and the time is not far distant when we shall purchase Canadian examples for our national and provincial collections."

This prediction was realized shortly after when Jackson's "Entrance to Halifax Harbor" was bought for the Tate Gallery.

From the United States came echoes of the same refrain. In the *International Interpreter,* a New York magazine devoted to the arts, a writer comments, "The strange thing is that these remote unsophisticated painters seem to have caught naturally the childlike vision that the sophisticated post-impressionists sought. . . Indeed there is not a poor, or weak, or derivative landscape here."

As in England the sincerity of the press's recognition was proven by the purchase of Jackson's canvas, so in the United States the head of the Pittsburg Art Gallery, after seeing the Canadian work at Wembley, opened a Canadian Section in the annual 1925 International exhibition, the most important yearly international art show held in America.

Opponents of the Group of Seven at home could not understand so much enthusiasm. "Flub-dub every word of it," wrote the indefatigable Hector Charlesworth in Toronto *Saturday Night.* "What some of us feared has come to pass. It was feared that the group of painters which elects to present in exaggerated terms the crudest and most sinister aspects of the Canadian wilds, would be accepted by the British critics as the most exclusive authentic interpreters of Canadian landscape. Whether as a result of a lobby or not, something like this has come to pass." Indeed, Mr. Eric Brown, curator of the Canadian National Gallery was criticised, because in compiling a booklet of press notices, only favourable ones appeared, the truth being that there were no unfavourable press comment except at home.

Some of the British writers, in looking for sources of influence in the group's work, suggested Russia, Scandinavia and even the Orient. In reply the Toronto *Star* said editorially, "The influence of our Canadian artists is Aztec and Iroquois, rather than Scandinavian or Oriental". Jackson's canvas purchased by the Tate Gallery was described as "a spilt can of paint." Charlesworth wrote, "There are no doubt parts of Canada which resemble parts of Russia, but a generalization about the scenery of Russia which has ports on the Black Sea, which extends to the North Pacific and which even in one corner breeds the largest and handsomest tigers known to naturalists, is as stupid as the belief that the interpreters of rocks and jackpines speak exclusively for present Canadian art."

But one Canadian periodical at least, the *Canadian Forum* did not miss the opportunity of pointing out that—the extent of the recognition in London was best illustrated by the list of pictures considered for purchase by the Tate Gallery trustees,—Tom Thomson's "West Wind", Arthur Lismer's "September Gale", J. E. H. MacDonald's "Beaver Dam", J. W. Morrice's "Beaupre" and A. Y. Jackson's "Entrance to Halifax Harbour". "This boils down," the *Forum* says, "to Morrice plus the Group of Seven. In the face of such evidence it is time for the blind antagonism of recent years to disappear, although there is plenty of room for severe criticism."

In referring to Wembley as a contributory incident to the spread of the movement, it is apropos to mention the recognition given by the English papers to a Montreal Group genealogically related to the Group of Seven movement. The names of some of its painters were mentioned in the early chapters of this book in relating the modernists' struggles in Montreal. As was then said, the modern artists in Montreal have kept in much closer touch with Europe than the modern movement in Toronto has. This has perhaps given to their work a more derivative quality, though possibly greater technical accomplishment.

An effort was made in Montreal to launch the "Beaver Hall Group" composed of Edwin Holgate,

Albert Robinson, Randolph Hewton, Clarence Gagnon, Mrs. Lilias Torrance Newton, Sarah Robertson, Anne Savage and Mabel May.

These Quebec painters are distinctly, though less aggressively, associated with the Canadian art movement of which this book is an appreciation. In 1925 Robinson exhibited with the Group of Seven in Toronto and in 1925 some of the lady members contributed canvases to a group show.

Randolph Hewton, from the days when he started exhibiting with Jackson, has been a disturbing element in the academic atmosphere of Montreal's art galleries. His fresh, lively portraits are a challenge to the professional practisers of the art whose works are widely known in the eastern city.

Robinson is a colourist who has no superior in Montreal. His bold designs and summaries have never pleased the critics, though when shown along with the work of the Seven in Toronto, they brought favourable comment. In some of his works, as in Jackson's, one is reminded of Morrice's qualities.

Holgate is both a pen draftsman and a painter. Whether painting or drawing, his work is robust and convincing. He seems pre-occupied with form rather than colour, and his pen drawings and engravings promise the opening up of a new avenue in Canadian art.

Clarence Gagnon for many years looked upon as our most accomplished etcher, has, for the past few years, been devoting himself to painting winter scenes in Quebec, which smack of the new spirit of Canadian art. His canvases are highly keyed and luminous and carefully enough finished so that he has never called down upon him the ire of the critic.

Of the ladies, Mrs. Newton's work has been in the portraits of women and children and she has received honourable mention at the Paris Salon. Mabel May, Sarah Robertson and Anne Savage are landscape painters who have made important contributions to modern work in Montreal. Miss Savage, as a teacher at the Baron Byng High School, has opened up a whole new vista of art training for children.

The Beaver Hall Group rented an old house for studios and started to work, but whether it was because the back woods never quite fired their creative genius, they did not, as a group, become an aggressive factor in Canadian art, though many of them individually have painted powerful canvases with the distinctive national note apparent in their Ontario contemporaries. Holgate, Hewton and Mrs. Newton as portrait painters, along with Varley of the Group of Seven, wrung enthusiastic praise from the British critics and Robinson, Gagnon and Hewton usually received mention in England bracketed with the names of their Toronto friends.

A member of the Seven to receive special mention in these Wembley discussions was F. H. Varley, whom we have referred to earlier as attracting the English critics in the War Memorial Exhibition in London in 1919, and who, because he is by preference a portrait, rather than a landscape painter, has not received the attention in this book that his friends have. The Canadian art movement has been distinctly confined to landscape and no claim can be made that it has seriously influenced portraiture, although Harris has digressed with success into this field and Holgate of Montreal has given us a portrait or two, which have a distinctively Canadian note in them.

Varley did, for a time, paint Canadian landscape in a way which showed that it had made a deep impression upon him. One of these early canvases, "Stormy Weather, Georgian Bay" was shown at Wembley. It depicted a fresh, breezy moment similar to the one which inspired Lismer's "September Gale", and was done near the same spot.

Varley is a painter with extraordinary talent and with great potential capacity for originality and feeling, but he is a sort of art gypsy. His best portraits have a fine knit quality with discerning characterization and fine conception. The draftsmanship is bold and the colour rich. He has painted many prominent Canadians and his portrait of Vincent Massey which hangs in Hart House, Toronto, was considered at the time it was done, the most modern piece of portraiture in the Dominion.

A nation will advance to meet its artists. This parable of the Group of Seven movement shows that when the soul of a man and the soul of his people and environment meet, the creative genius of a race bursts into flame. But that is only a beginning of a road without an end. The creative genius of a race or of a man lies in the capacity to respond to the finer things of life,—love of nature, love of home, love of people as a whole, love of contact with great minds and great hearts in the painting, poetry and music of all peoples and all ages, and the love of beauty for its own sake. The denial of this creative genius, national or individual, is the denial of that spirit in man for which the New Testament says there is no forgiveness—forgiveness being freedom.

The message that the Group of Seven art movement gives to this age is the message that here in the North has arisen a young nation with faith in its own creative genius. British North America in the first fifty years of its confederation gave indication of such a faith in almost all fields except the creative arts. Culturally it chose to remain a mere outpost of Europe. To-day, so far as painting is concerned this is no longer true. At home the significance of it dawns slowly. The significance will appear as Canadian genius becomes respected abroad. When the genius of other lands is drawn to us for inspiration instead of ours being drawn to the old well-mellowed cultures of Europe, then will the fetters of the past be struck off, and we shall know that "the sweetest songs yet remain to be sung."

SOME WORKS OF THE GROUP OF SEVEN IN PUBLIC COLLECTIONS.

MacDonald, J. E. H.

Winter Moonlight ....The Grange, Toronto.
Beaver Dam ....The Grange, Toronto.
Solemn Land ....National Gallery, Ottawa.
Nova Scotia Coast ....National Gallery, Ottawa.
Cattle and Stream ....National Gallery, Ottawa.
March Evening, Northland ...National Gallery, Ottawa.
Winter Morning ....Ontario Government.

Lismer, Arthur

September Gale ....National Gallery, Ottawa.
Guides' Home ....National Gallery, Ottawa.
Winter Camouflage ....National Gallery, Ottawa.
Road Through the Bush ......National Gallery, Ottawa.
West Wind ....National Gallery, Ottawa.
Bon Echo ....National Gallery, Ottawa.
The Clearing ....Normal School, Ottawa.
Nova Scotia River ....Nova Scotia Museum of Fine Arts, Halifax.

Carmichael, Frank

Snow Clouds....................Hart House, Toronto.
Jackfish Village ....The Grange, Toronto.
October ....National Gallery, Ottawa.

Jackson, A. Y.

Entrance to Halifax Harbour.Tate Gallery, London.
November, Georgian Bay ....Hart House, Toronto.
Maples, Early Spring ....Sarnia Library, Sarnia, Ont.
Early Spring, Quebec ....National Gallery, Ottawa.
Night, Georgian Bay ....National Gallery, Ottawa.
November, Lake Superior ......National Gallery, Ottawa.
Red Maple ....National Gallery, Ottawa.
Winter Moonlight ....Kitchener, Ontario.

HARRIS, LAWREN

MORNING SUN, WINTER	Detroit Art Gallery, Detroit, Mich.
THE CORNER STORE	The Grange, Toronto.
HOUSE IN SNOWSTORM	The Grange, Toronto.
AFTERNOON SUN, LAKE SUPERIOR.	National Gallery, Ottawa.
SNOW PATTERN	National Gallery, Ottawa.
PINES, KEMPENFELDT BAY	National Gallery, Ottawa.
SHACKS, WINTER	National Gallery, Ottawa.
WINTER, ALGONQUIN PARK	National Gallery, Ottawa.
DECORATIVE LANDSCAPE	Y.W.C.A., Toronto.
TREES IN AUTUMN, ALGOMA	Women's Union, University of Toronto.

SOME CANVASES BY TOM THOMSON IN PUBLIC COLLECTIONS*

NOVEMBER	Sarnia Library, Sarnia, Ont.
MORNING CANOE	Sarnia Library, Sarnia, Ont.
THE DRIVE	Ontario Agricultural College, Guelph.
WEST WIND	The Grange, Toronto.
NORTHERN LAKE	Normal School, Ottawa.
NORTHERN RIVER	National Gallery, Ottawa.
JACK PINE	National Gallery, Ottawa.
SPRING ICE	National Gallery, Ottawa.
THE GARLAND	National Gallery, Ottawa.

*Tom Thomson was, strictly speaking, never a member of the Group of Seven.

Index

A

"Above Lake Superior" (canvas), 188.
A. E. (George Russell), 38.
Algoma, 137, 148, 158, 159, 161, 187.
Algonquin Park, 28, 95, 116, 123.
Allan, Mrs. Andrew, 68, 106.
Arts and Letters Club, Toronto, 38, 57, 92.

B

Bakst, Leon, 189.
Barbeau, C. M., 203.
Beatty, J. W., 41, 45, 46, 95, 124.
Beaverbrook, Lord, 128.
Beaver Hall Group, 211, 213.
Bell, Clive, 21.
"Black Court" (canvas), 185.
Box-car Party, 138.
Bridle, Augustus, 44, 45, 47, 158.
Broadhead, Wm., 25, 60.
Brockville, Ont., 206.
Brown, Eric, 58, 210.
Brymner, Wm., 68.

C

Canadian Bookman, 12, 20, 43, 173, 196.
Canadian Courier, 40, 44, 45.
Canadian Forum, 22, 144, 150, 197, 210.
Canadian Magazine, 61.
Canadian National Gallery, 19, 59, 76, 88, 89, 177.
Canadian Theosophist, 13.
Canadian War Records, 107, 128, 163.
Carmichael, Frank, 25, 31, 60, 99, 104, 110, 197, 199.
Casson, Alfred J., 146.
Catalogue, Group of Seven, 157.
Charlesworth, Hector, 109, 209, 210.
Chatham, 205.
Chez Nous, 168.
Christian Science Monitor, 99.
Cullen, Maurice, 20, 23, 55.

D

Daily Chronicle, 208.
Daily Telegraph, 133.
Donovan, Peter, 93.

E

"Elevator Court" (canvas), 185.
"Entrance to Halifax Harbour" (canvas), 124, 163.
"Edge of the Maple Wood" (canvas), 54, 77, 84.

F

Fairley, Barker, 144.
Faure, Elie, 16.
Field, The, 208.
"First Snow Ducks" (canvas), 117, 121.
Fort William, Ont., 205.
Fry, Roger, 152.

G

Gadsby, H. F., 93.
Gagnon, Clarence, 53, 55, 212.
Georgian Bay, 39, 54, 60, 83, 164, 177.
Globe, The, 65, 112.

Go Home Bay, 39, 86, 87.
Grange, The, 58, 120, 157.
Grip Limited, 25, 45, 60.
Group of Seven, 97, 143, 204.

H

Halifax, N.S., 163, 172, 185.
"Happy Isles" (canvas), 179.
Harris, Lawren, 34, 35, 47, 63, 64, 65, 77, 82, 99, 136, 161, 182, 188, 193.
Hewton, R. S., 68, 69, 71, 72, 76, 106, 212.
Holgate, Edwin, 211.

I

International Interpreter, 150, 209.
"Islands of Spruce" (canvas), 178.

J

"Jack Pine" (canvas), 120.
Jackson, A. Y., 21, 50, 57, 67, 68, 69, 70, 72, 76, 82, 91, 96, 99, 103, 104, 106, 126, 128, 150, 163, 193, 201.
Jefferys, C. W., 48.
Johnston, Frank, 25, 31, 138, 158.
Julien's Academy, 53.

K

Kane, Paul, 19.
Kreighoff, Cornelius, 19.
Konody, Paul, 130.
Kyle, Fergus, 65.

L

Lake Superior, North shore, 187.
Lamb, H. Mortimer, 73, 81, 205.
Lamps, The, 128, 139.
Laval, Monseigneur de, 18.
Lismer, Arthur, 13, 25, 30, 32, 41, 46, 60, 61, 63, 99, 107, 117, 172.
Luc, Frère, 18.
Lyman, J. G., 68, 71, 106.

M

MacCallum, Dr. J. M., 38, 61, 66, 85.
MacDonald, J. E. H., 25, 26, 38, 40, 47, 61, 63, 64, 76, 91, 95, 99, 107, 124, 132, 139, 143, 160, 195, 201.
MacGregor Bay, Ont., 179.
Mail & Empire, 159.
Maligne Lake (canvas), 197.
Massey, Vincent (portrait), 215.
Mattawa, Ont., 173.
May, Mabel, 212.
McKechnie, Neil, 25, 125.
McLean, Tom, 25, 41.
Montreal Art Association, 70.
Montreal *Standard,* The, 82.
Montreal *Star,* The, 70, 72, 81.
Montreal *Witness,* The, 71.
Morning Post, The, 11, 17, 208.
"Mountain Forms" (canvas), 197.
Morrice, J. W., 20, 55, 71.

N

Nation, The, 133.
New Statesman, The, 143.
Newton, Mrs. Lilias Torrance, 212.
"Northern Lake" (canvas), 62.
"Northern River" (canvas), 99.

O

Ontario College of Art, 58.
Ontario Society of Artists, 27, 36, 40, 44, 45, 47, 57, 62, 99, 107, 144.
Owen Sound, Ont., 205.

P

Paul, St. Vincent de, 18.
Philadelphia, Pa., 207.
Pittsburgh, Pa., 209.
Port Arthur, Ont., 205.
Powell, Morgan, 70, 71, 72.

INDEX

Q

Quebec, Province of, 167, 173, 201, 212.
Quevillon, Louis, 18.

R

Rebel, The, 125, 132.
Robertson, Sarah, 212.
Robinson, A. H., 55.
Robson, A. H., 25, 60.
Rocky Mountains, 95, 193.
Royal Canadian Academy, 45, 69, 101.
Royal Ontario Museum, 19.

S

Sarnia, Ont., 121, 205.
Saturday Night, 109, 209.
Savage, Anne, 212.
Scandinavian Art, 63.
"September Gale" (canvas), 153, 176.
Smith, Goldwin, 58.
"Solemn Land" (canvas), 160.
"Stormy Weather, Georgian Bay" (canvas), 214.
Studio Building for Canadian Art, 66, 84, 115.

T

"Tangled Garden, The" (canvas), 107, 112.
Tate Gallery, The, 163, 204.
Thomson, Tom, 25, 28, 40, 46, 60, 61, 63, 67, 91, 99, 115.
Toronto Star, 93, 108, 155, 210.
Trail, The (Alta.), 205.

U

United States, 82, 206.

V

Vancouver, 205.
Van Horne, Sir Wm., 50.
Varley, F. H., 25, 31, 128, 196, 213, 214.

W

Walker, Sir Edmund, 59, 79, 128.
War Memorials Exhibition, 131.
Wembley, 109, 204, 207.
"West Wind" (canvas), 117, 119.
Whitman, Walt, 17, 65, 97, 122.
"Wild River" (canvas), 159.
"Winter Road" (canvas), 170.

Y

Year Book of Canadian Art, 12, 58, 63, 65, 72.

Hudson Bay
North Shore
Laurentians
L. Superior
Algoma
Algonquin Park
Georgian Bay
L. Simcoe
Toronto
L. Ontario
J·M·

DATE DUE

BRODART Cat. No. 23-221